Hugh Malcolm Roberts was born on 3rd January 1945, in Birmingham, the second child to William and Amy Roberts whose first son John had died aged thirteen on 15th December 1943. Following the death of his father on 13th June 1963, while searching through his papers, he discovered a small paper bag which contained a pocket address book and many scraps of paper. These turned out to be the diary of his time in the Great War. Fifty-three years later, having retired the previous year, Hugh began the challenging task of transcribing them into this book. As can be seen within the text, William's writing is very small and hence the need to make regular use of a magnifying glass!

Hugh left school in the summer of 1961 and secured a position as a trainee quantity surveyor. This led to his attaining qualification as a chartered surveyor and later, having switched careers in 1977, as a chartered loss adjuster. Between these two choices came a period of working in Jamaica and London before a return to the second city and the move to loss adjusting. Upon qualifying in this second career, promotion followed together with a move to Cheltenham where he now lives.

Upon the one hundredth anniversary of the outbreak of the First World War in 2014, Hugh was interviewed by the BBC for both television and radio when he took the opportunity of explaining not only his father's role in that conflict but also that of his regiment, The Durham Light Infantry.

DEDICATION

This work is dedicated to those brave souls of The Durham Light Infantry who, along with my father, fought to keep their country free from tyranny in arduous conditions on the Western Front during the years 1914 to 1918. Not forgotten are their comrades who did likewise in other theatres of the conflict throughout the globe.

Hugh Malcolm Roberts

THE GREAT SURVIVOR

AUSTIN MACAULEY PUBLISHERS™
LONDON • CAMBRIDGE • NEW YORK • SHARJAH

A CIP catalogue record for this title is available from the British Library.

ISBN 9781787105003 (Paperback)
ISBN 9781788233736 (Hardback)
ISBN 9781788233743 (ePub e-book)

www.austinmacauley.com

First Published (2021)
Austin Macauley Publishers Ltd
25 Canada Square
Canary Wharf
London
E14 5LQ

ACKNOWLEDGEMENTS

I should like to express my thanks to the following for their kind assistance in my task of compiling this transcription.

Fred Ashmore whose knowledge of the Battle of The Aisne was invaluable.

David Blanchard who guided me to the records of my father's entry to the POW camps.

Sean Godfrey who 'kick started' the whole thing.

Colin Penman whose encyclopaedic knowledge of computers helped in resolving my numerous 'dead ends'.

Peter Simkins who also provided guidance which enabled me to begin.

John McLaren, for his guidance and advice in respect of important items, such as the wording for the cover.

EDITOR'S NOTE

Throughout, I have transcribed the writing precisely including any spelling or grammatical errors. Curved brackets are my father's: straight brackets are mine.

CONTENTS

INTRODUCTION

William John Glanvor Roberts was born on 21st April 1894 in Llangefni, the capital of the Isle of Anglesey. The small terrace of five cottages was at right angles to the main road through the centre and were demolished circa 2006 to facilitate a new access road to an Asda supermarket. I visited shortly after this was carried out.

He was one of thirteen children, only five of whom survived to adulthood, when he became the eldest.

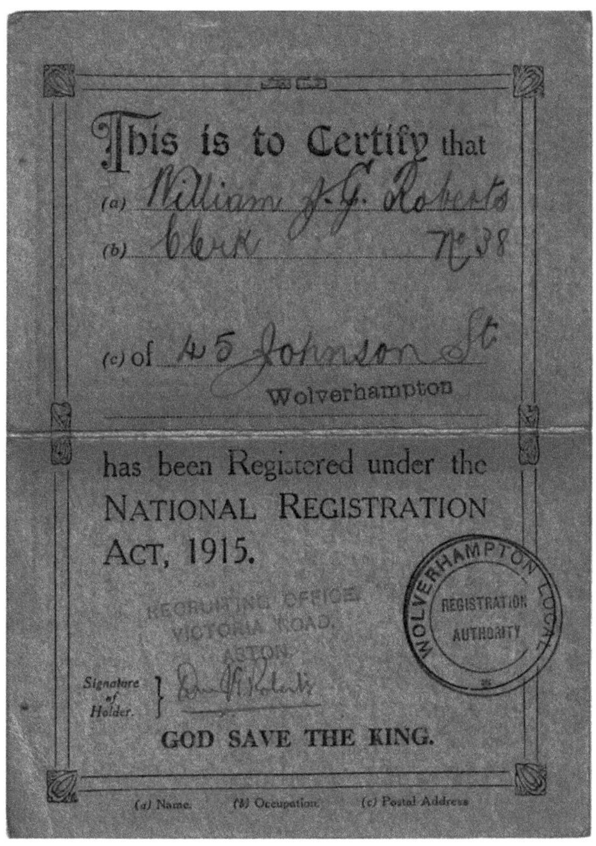

This is to Certify that

(a) William J. G. Roberts

(b) Clerk No 38

(c) of 45 Johnson St

Wolverhampton

has been Registered under the NATIONAL REGISTRATION ACT, 1915.

RECRUITING OFFICE, VICTORIA ROAD, ASTON.

WOLVERHAMPTON LOCAL REGISTRATION AUTHORITY

Signature of Holder.

GOD SAVE THE KING.

(a) Name. (b) Occupation. (c) Postal Address

His father, James had moved to Anglesey from Ruthin in Denbighshire circa 1889-90 and also inhabited Llangefni where he worked as a saddler. Following the invention of the motorcar, the opportunities for saddlers diminished and so when my father was about thirteen James moved the family to Wolverhampton where he gained employment with the Standard Motor Company as an upholsterer.

William succeeded well at school and became an accountant, working in nearby Birmingham when war was declared in 1914. He volunteered at the outbreak but although being recruited was excused being called up due to his being considered by the authorities to be in a deferred occupation under the Derby Scheme. In 1915 the government introduced identity cards: that for my father is included above.

However, because of the substantial losses incurred, in 1916 he was called to duty and enlisted in the Durham Light Infantry. Apparently this geographical anomaly resulted from the DLI having suffered significant losses in manpower in consequence of which men were recruited from all corners of the country.

William began his training at Doncaster barracks circa July 1916 and from there the diaries continue.

Below is a transcript of Particulars given to the Demob Officer on 5th August 1919 when he was 25 years of age and residing in Wolverhampton (45 Johnston Street).

- **Enlisted 12.12.15**
- **England 12.12.15-4.8.17**
- **France 4.8.17-15.10.17**
- **England 15.10.17-17.2.18**
- **France 17.2.18-27.5.18**
- **Germany 27.5.18-15.12.18**
- **England 15.12.18-**

The above appears to be a very abbreviated list because it does not account for his time in Flanders [his reference to France for that period may be a mistake] when he fought in the Third Battle of Ypres at Polygon Wood in October 1917. The return to England on 15.10.17 represents his having been wounded in that battle and the wound being of a severity such that he could not be treated in either one of the casualty clearing stations or a field hospital.

The transcript continues:–

Cash instead of S???
Cash instead of S???
Gunshot wounds in Left Knee.
Nervous Debility.
Defective Eyesight.
W.J.G-1894 – 25 – Wolverhampton.[1]

What follows is a transcription of a list of dates and activities not entered in a formal diary.

20/1/14 Commenced biz at Mid Hotel Bm.[2]

4/4/14 Fell ill when with Howard in Broad Street & went to Dr Gordon Hackney. Went back to Midland to bed.

5/4/14 Dr called and said I needed operation. Arranged for me to go to Queens Hosp. at 3 o'c. Mr Stephens went with me.

6/4/14 Dr Billingham operated.

12/4/14 Elsie called to see me.

21/4/14[3] **Left the hospital. Mr Stephens came to see me away to New St. Station in taxi.**

11/4/14 Commenced biz at Midland.[4]

14/4/14 Went to Wn.[5]

18/4/14 Went to Cheltenham.[6]

6/7/14 Went to Boxing at Sparkbrook had introduction to Jerry Delaney, Frank Delaney, Jimmy Wilde & his manager & other boxing celebrities.

1 I believe that this conveys his date of birth and place of residence.

2 He was an accountant and worked in the hotel business both before WW1 and after, when he progressed to management.

3 This entry is smudged and appears to be out of date order. This would have been on his 20th birthday.

4 From memory of what my mother told me, the operation could have been for peritonitis and may explain his being disorientated.

5 This appears to be a visit to his home in Wolverhampton.

6 Where I now live (2016).

3/7/14[7] Met Winnie Holmes for 1st time.

18/7/14 Met Doris at Flower show.

4/8/14 England declared war on Germany at midnight.

4/9/14 Went to Teignmouth with Howard.

12/9/14 Returned to Bm. Called at Recruiting Office. (Council House).[8]

30/1/15 Gordon left Midland[Hotel] and Ritoen took over.

17/4/15 Left Midland Hotel. Went into digs in Westminster Road.

19/4/15 Commenced business at Kelseys [Brewery?].

7/5/15 Lusitania sunk by submarine.

5/6/15 Moved from Westminster Road to Hartwells.

10/7/15 Went to Teignmouth.[9]

17/7/15 Retn from do.

22/8/15 Howard, Elsie& Rene & myself baptized by the Rev S W Hughes at Christ Church Six Ways Aston.

29/8/15 Mr Hughes' last Sund. at Christ Ch.

7 Another out of sequence, or was it 13th?

8 Where in 1926/7 my mother was working as a secretary when he met her.

9 The address book included within the bundle of papers forming the diary contains an entry for a female friend.

On the rear of the above sheet is the following list (presumably of persons known to WJGR):-

- Miss Irene Bragg, 106, Heathfield Road.
- Miss Lilly Savage, 88, Heathfield Road.
- Simian Burrows, Lake House, Lake Street, Lower Gornal, Nr Dudley, Staffs.
- Notes on Film Developing & other interesting notes. Notes 1917 No.1)
- Mabel 21st June 1886.
- Euginie High St. Erd.[Erdington Birmingham?]
- Albert 5th Jan. 1895.
- Howard Sutton Rd. Erd.
- Alice 10th March 1889.
- Gertrude 64 Lich Rd. [Lichfield?]
- Annie 12th Oct. 1896.
- Eloie
- Victoria High St. Erd.

Next in the bundle are two sheets in another's hand writing which are difficult to decipher:-

Oct. 1914.

1 Bar BA Costs nearly	1.5.0
1 Bar BA	2.8.0
30% disc.	14.6 nearly
	1.13.6
Costs	1. 5.0
	8.6 profit
1 Bar x Costs	19.4
1 Bar x Costs	19.4
	1 Bar x 1.16.0
	30% disc nearly 10.10
	1.15.2
Costs	19.4
	5.10 profit

Nov 1915

1 Bar BA Costs	nearly 2.6.0
1 Bar BA	2.8.0
30% disc	nearly 14.6
	1.13.6
	+ War Tax 19.0
	2.12.6
	Costs 2.6.0
	6.6 profit
1 Bar x Costs	nearly 1.18.6
	1 Bar x 1.16.0
30% disc	nearly 10.10
	1.5.2
+ War Tax	19.2
	2.4.2
	Costs 1.18.6
	5.8 profit

TRAINING, FLANDERS AND FRANCE

On the rear of the photographs below are notes indicating that he was undergoing training at Doncaster on 16th July 1916. The next entry in the diary is not until early August 1917 as can be seen from the continuation: I can only interpret that he remained in training [with leave] or was posted elsewhere [possibly in Europe] during the intervening period. [When I was very young he whispered in my ear one day about his time in the war and that he had been on the Somme but this may have been a reference to his time in that area training for Polygon Wood in the summer of 1917 to which he refers in the diary.]

Below are four photographs of my father with his platoon while undergoing training at Doncaster on 16th July 1916. On the reverse are his handwritten annotations to this effect, the one for the soldier with the moustache says: **'W. Ward. Doncaster 16.7.16 (Killed at Ypres 1917)'**. He is sitting at the extreme left of the front row [in the photograph of ten men] with my father on his left. There is no comment to identify the others.

Private W J G Roberts

The following is from notes made prior to his departure to and arrival in France.

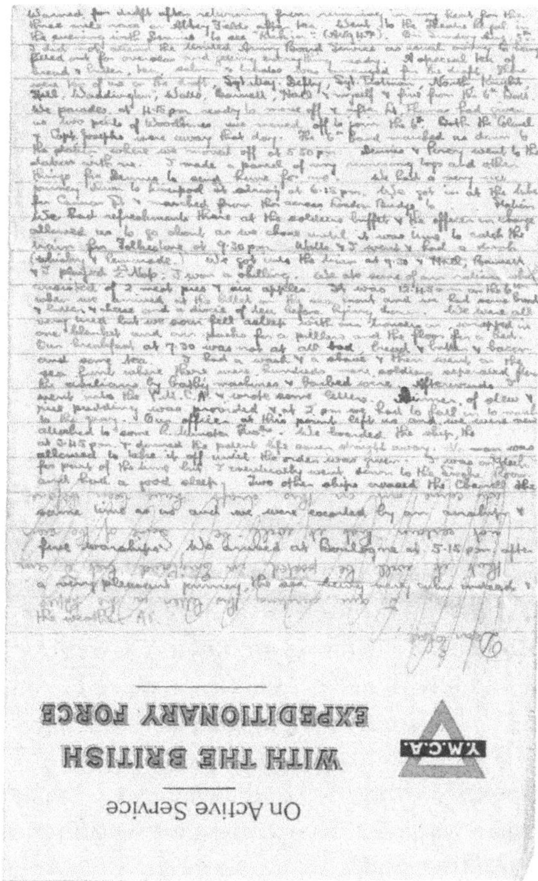

Warmed for draft after returning from running in my heat for the three mile race on Abbey Fields after tea. Went to the theatre Royal in the evening with Dennis to see "Kick In" (Aug 4th). On Sunday Aug 5th I did not attend the United Army Board Service as usual owing to being fitted out for overseas and getting everything ready. A special tea of bread and butter, tea, salmon and tomato arranged for the draft. There were ten of us on the draft; Sgt. Maj. Defty, Sgt. Trotman, North, Knight, Hall, Waddington, Watts, Connell, Hall and myself & five from the 6th Batt.[10]

10 I assume that the year is 1916.

We parades at 4.15pm ready to move off & after Lt. Thomas had given us two pkts of Woodbines we moved off to join the 6th.[11] Both the Colonel & Capt. Josephs were away that day. The 6th band marched us down to the station where we moved off at 5.50pm. Dennis & Percy went to the station with me.

I made a parcel of my running togs and other things for Dennis to send home for me. We had a very nice journey down to Liverpool St. arriving at 6.15pm. We got in at the tube for Cannon St. & marched from this across London Bridge to [Charing Cross, Waterloo?]................. Station. We had refreshments there at the soldiers' buffet & the officer in charge allowed us to go about as we chose until it was time to catch the train for Folkestone at 9.30pm. Watts & I went and had a drink (Whisky & lemonade).We got into the train at 9.30 & Hall, Barnett & I played 1/2d Nap; I won a shilling. We ate some of our rations which consisted of 2 meat pies & six apples. It was 12.45am on the 6th when we arrived at the billet on the sea front and we had some bread & butter & cheese and a dixie of tea before lying down. We were all very tired but we soon fell asleep with our trousers on, wrapped in one blanket and our packs for a pillow and the floor for a bed.

Our breakfast at 7.30 was not at all bad; bread & butter & bacon and some tea. I had a wash & a shave & then went on the sea front where there were hundreds more soldiers separated from the civilians by bathing machines & barbed wire. Afterwards I went into the Y.M.C.A. & wrote some letters. Dinner of stew & rice pudding was provided & at 2pm we had to fall in to march to the quay. Our officer at this point left us and we were now attached to some R. Munster Fusiliers. We boarded the ship, the.................[12] at 3.45 & donned the patent life saver straight away. No man was allowed to take it off until the order was given. I was on deck for part of the time but I eventually went down to the Smoke Room and had a good sleep.

11 At this juncture I would add that my father progressed through five or six battalions due to him eventually being wounded more than once and returned to the UK each time and after being brought back to health returning to a new training battalion and further battalions in Flanders and France.

12 Name not inserted.

Two other ships crossed the Channel the same time as us and we were escorted by an airship & five warships. We arrived at Boulogne at 5.15pm after a very pleasant journey, the sea being very calm indeed.

There is then a summary:– [I interpret that the gaps in times etc. are the result of his failed intention to enter them at a later time]

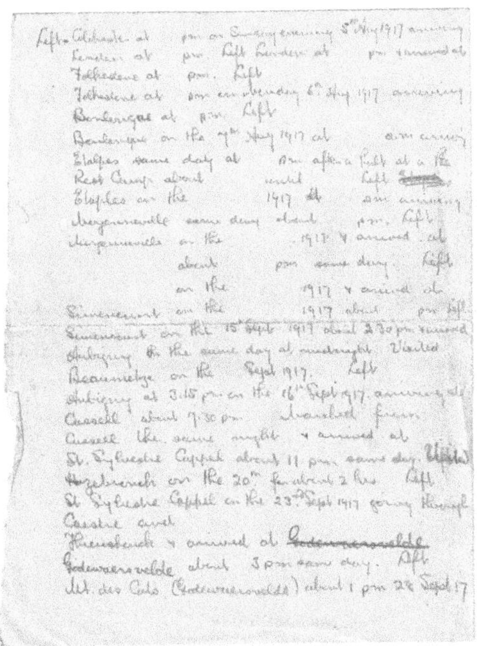

Left: Colchester at pm on Sunday evening 5th Aug 1917 arriving London at pm. Left London at pm & arrived at Folkestone at pm. Left Folkestone at pm on Monday 6th Aug 1917 arriving Boulogne at pm. Left Boulogne on the 7th Aug 1917 at am arriving Etalpes[13] same day at pm after a halt at a Rest Camp about until .

Left:Etaples on the 1917 at am arriving Bayonneville same day about pm.

Left Bayonneville on the 1917 & arrived at About pm same day. Left on the 1917 and arrived at Simoncourt on the 1917 about pm. Left

13 Étaples; his spelling.

Simoncourt on the 15th Sept 1917 about 2.30 pm & arrived Aubigny on the same day at midnight. Visited Beaumetze on the Sept 1917. Left Aubigny at 3.15 pm on the 16th Sept 1917 arriving at Cassell about 7.30 pm. ????? from Cassell the same night & arrived at St. Sylvestre Cappel about 11 pm same day. Visited Hazebrouck on the 20th for about 2 hrs. Left St. Sylvestre Cappel on the 23rd Sept 1917 going through Caestre and Thieushouck & arrived at Godewaersvelde about 3 pm same day. Left Mt. des Cols (Godewaersvelde) about 1 pm 28 Sept 17.

There follows a transcript of some poetry from 1900 and 1917 although the sources are not stated.

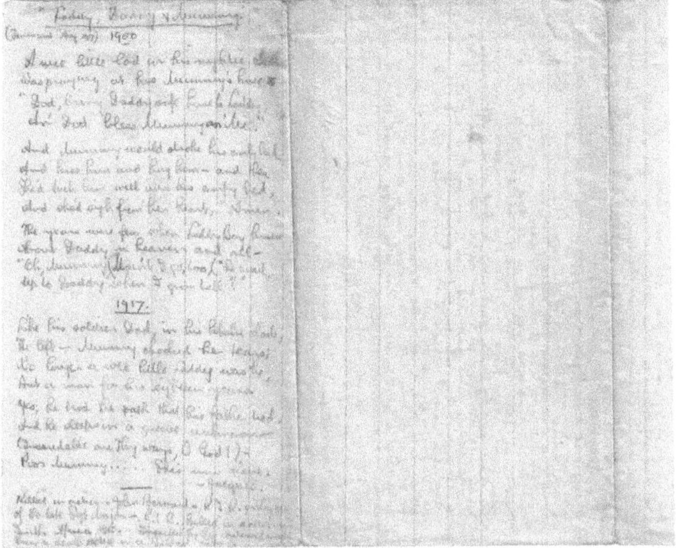

1900

"Laddy, Daddy & Mummy" (Forward Aug 1917)

A wee little lad in his nightie cloths,
Was praying at his Mummy's knee,
"Dod, bring Daddy safe home to Laddy,
An Dod bless Mummy an' He".

And Mummy would stroke his curly head
And kiss him and hug him – and then
She'd tuck him well into his comfy bed,
And she'd sigh from her heart, "Amen".

The years were few when Laddy Boy knew
About Daddy in heaven and all –
"Oh mummy Main't I go too (he cried)'
Up to Daddy when I grow tall?".

1917

Like his soldier Dad, in his khaki clad,
He left – Mummy checked her tears;
No longer a wee little Laddy was he,
But a man for his eighteen years.

Yes; he trod the path that his father had,
And he sleeps in a grave unknown –
(Inscrutable are Thy ways, O God!) –
Poor Mummy……………She's now alone.

Jacques.

Killed in action – John Bernard – R.I.P., only son of the late Sgt. Major – R.I.P. killed in action in South Africa, 1900. Inserted by his widowed mother from a death notice in a Belfast paper.

There is then the cover of a notebook on the inside of which is the following scroll hand written by my father:

This appears to have been opened following his arrival in France and, as will become clear later, received entries on a spasmodic basis as time would allow. Consequently, the dates that follow may not be strictly chronological in order.

The first page notes:–

Committee Parcels (conserves)

Packed and despatched by Messrs. Morten & Co. under authority granted by the Central Prisoners of War Committee of the Brit. Red Cross Society & the Order of St. John of Jerusalem in England.

British Kiaegskefaugenener,

The President, Brit. Help Cmte., Lager Lechfeld, Bavaria, Germany.

Biscuits.

Bureau De Secours,Aux Prisonniers De Guerre, Section Anglais, Berne, Switzerland.

The next page [reverse of the previous page] is reproduced below:–

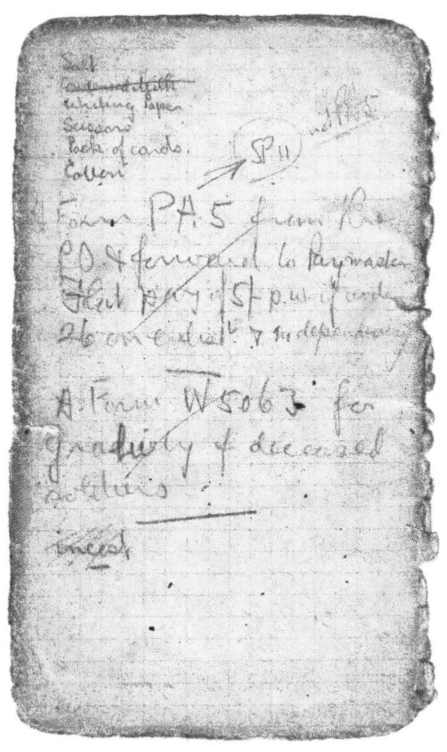

Salt
Writing Paper
Scissors
Pack of cards.
Collars
SP11
Form PA 5 from the
C.O. & forward to Paymaster
A Form W5063 for
gratuity of deceased
soldiers

Leaving the notebook for now we return to the separate pages and September 1917.

14th Sept 1917. Started on new job as Company clerk. Footer match in the evening between 10th K.O.Y.L.I. s & 15th D.L.I. for final of Bgde. Competition. D.L.I. won 5-2.

15th Sept. 1917. Left Simoncourt at 5.30pm and after a long march arrived at Aubigny o/n at 12pm.[14] Only "A" Coy came away. Acted as loading

14 He might mean midnight.

party for the Brigade. I helped with the loading for some time but slept during the night. Capt. Saunders in charge of the Coy lost his way several times during the journey. Slept in one of the huts used as a hospital during the night. An officer of the R.A.M.C. came in & lay on the table. He had been travelling for 36 hrs. *after* coming out of the trenches & had had no sleep. He was on his way home on leave but he missed the night's leave train.

16th Sept. 1917. Bfast, a biscuit & a bit of bacon. Did nothing during the morning. B.C.&D. Companies arrived at the station & left Aubigny at 12.30pm. A. Coy left at 3.15pm arriving at Cassell station about 7.30pm. Had a rotten march from there to St Sylvestre Cappel. Capt. Saunders lost his way again. Charlie, Atkins, Major & Quarter & myself billeted in a barn for the night. Had some bread & butter from the farm house for supper. Major paid.

17th,18th. Did very little these two days.

19th. Went on parade with Holyerts[?][Mt. de Cats?] Platoon for "New Advance" manoeuvres. I acted as Runner for Lieut. Sedgewick. Stores shifted from the barn to a cowshed. Very much nicer place. Charlie, Atkins & myself sleep in the stores. Major & Quarter sleep in the farmhouse.

20th. Went to Hazebrouck in the evening. Bought several things; pipe, note book, pencil & had one or two drinks with Watts & Waddington.

21st& 22nd. Had a quiet time. Did some washing on the Friday.

23rd(Sunday). Left St. Sylvestre Cappel with full pack & marched through Caestre & Thieushouck to Godewaersvelde. Had the stores in a cowshed. Major, Quarter, Charlie, Atkins & myself slept in the stores. Atkins & myself cleaned the place out. Had dinner on field at Thieushouck.

24th. Went for a route march in the morning. Had the pack on for 1 ½ hours without a ????? [spell?]

25th. Marched with full marching order to Batt. Hdqtrs. For inspection by Major Bowsfield. Had to parade at 5 o'clock for inspectn by C.C.O. Pay at 6. Went down to the village with Charlie Renwick a[fter] pay. Not same silk post sends. [???] Went to a café and had some eggs, bread & butter & tea. (1fr 30.). Disturbance on in the Camp 7 a[fter] Lights Out. (see amended slip).

Tuesday 25th September 1917._A disturbance was provoked in the Company after Lights Out which almost turned to mutiny. The C.S.M. went into the barn where the men were sleeping and warned them that no more lights were to be lit and that if they wanted to talk they must talk quietly. He hadn't gone far away when a light was lit & he went inside the barn & took the man's name. This seemed to have disturbed the men & they started chattering & talking loudly and the S.M. warned them again that it must cease otherwise he would see the Captain about punishing them by giving them a three hours route march on the morrow. This quietened the majority of the men & Cpls. & Lefts. ordered the others to shut up but that only made things worse. The Major had gone out but came in again & took some more names this time for making a noise. The men seemed to be getting roused more & more & one man, Pvte. D. Brown, was more impudent than the others & was eventually placed under close arrest in the quad-room. He was ordered to give up cigarettes & matches rc by the S.M. but refused in insolent style. All this caused a great commotion & the other men seemed furious & shouted and hooted, one man suggesting that they should put the S.M. in the pond. It was a great disturbance & mutiny was narrowly averted. The men quietened down about 11.30 pm & nothing more happened. The company was not punished & D. Brown only got 7 days C.B. & a good talking to when he came before Capt. Saunders in the morning.

26th. Night Manoevres at 9 o'c. Nothing doing during the day.

27th. Quiet day.

28th Sept. 1917. Left Mt. des Cals in Godewaersvelde about 1 o'c pm and a(fter) a very gruelling march arrived at .... 3.5 klms from Di........... about 5.30 pm absolutely whacked. Hallisnan (Halliman? Alleyman?) active in the evening dropped several bombs in the vicinity. Slept in Hdqrs. Hut. No room in the stores.

29th. Lecture by Brigadier in the evening. Halliman[15] again active & dropped bombs in galore. Many casualties & O as he appeared passing the moon. Went to the Y.M.C.A. with Watts & Waddington.

30th. Fritz over in his aeroplanes again & dropped a number of bombs in the neighbourhood. His manoeuvring was very interesting to watch especially as he foreclosed in the moonlight.

1917 Oct 1st Monday – Oct 4th Thursday. I was busy in the morning writing out different Rolls for the C.S.M. & eventually the Major had to stay back with the Nucleus. I packed my packs ready for the transport at 1 o'c. I had a good dinner with the Major, Quarter, Charlie & Hack & paraded with Hdqtrs' platoon about 2.30 pm for moving off. It was a tiring journey all the way from Sherpenberg Camp to the place we eventually arrived at. The first halt we had was close to a cemetery & a burying party was busy at the time. On arriving at the camp we got some iron bars, wire & a sheet & put up a bivouac for the four of us. Charlie, Hack, the Quarter & myself. I wrote a letter to Elsie for Hack to post in Blighty. Tea was very welcomed on our arrival or soon afterwards at least. Halliman was over in the evening dropping bombs but I got down to it very early. We drew our packs before tea so had our great coats to put over us at night besides the 2 or 3 blankets which we had bet.n us. Bfast, dinner & tea were thoroughly enjoyed the next day.

Tuesday and I rested as much as possible. Valises were packed up again for the transport but this time overcoats were left out. We carried them up the line rolled round the haver-sack. I broke my new pipe, one I had bought at Hasbrouck, just a(fter) tea and had to go & get another one from my pack to take up with me. We had a very good view of the Observation Balloons at this place & saw them descending & ascending. Six o'clock was a great moment when we all fell in ready to start for the final stopping place. The facial expressions were very numerous, but on the whole everyone was very steady. The men's loads were very heavy, in fact much too heavy for fighting purposes. I carried 220 rounds of ammunition, 4 Mills bombs besides ordinary equipment and a full haversack, made full by the extra rations which Charlie gave me to take up with me. We marched off in fours but as soon as we got on

15 This could be 'Alleyman', i.e. a standard name for German of the time. (From the French, *allemand*.)

the Ypres Road we formed two deep. I don't think any order was given but the condition of the road necessitated it. The marching as regards step &c was very poor all the way but the weight we were carrying was absolutely ridiculous.[16] It was quite dark a(fter) we had been marching for half an hour and somehow some strange troops got mixed with the Batt. & we halted at the first turning for them to get clear.

There follows a listing by my father of events between 4th October 1917 and 26th January 1918. This is written on the reverse side of a Y.M.C.A. note sheet, both sides of which are illustrated below. I now transcribe the chronology.

1917

Oct 4th. Wounded in Polygon Wood. Removed to clearing station at Poperhinge.[17]

Oct 5th. Moved to hosp. at Godewaersvelde.

Oct 7th. Moved from Godewaersvelde.

Oct 8th. Arrived at 20th Gen. Hosp. at Carniens.[18]

Recuperation

Oct 14th&15th Left Carniers at midnight on the 14th for Calais & sailed from there on the 15th[19] at Dover. Left Dover 4.30 pm.

Oct 16th Arrived at Merryflats W.H., Govan, Glasgow at 4.30 am.

? Oct 1917 Went to a party in the afternoon given by Church people in Glasgow. Had a fairly good time. Very good tea provided & plenty of cigarettes. Games were held & I entered for the "Frog Leaping" & "Hat

16 My father was not a big man. I am 5'6"and he was smaller.

17 His medical record states 'Gunshot wound to the knee'.

18 Carniers?

19 Later in the diaries under the heading The Notebook is an image of his Pay record. At the top of that page is the comment: 'Sailed across on Mond Oct 15/17 in the "Pietre de Coningle"'.

Trimming". Three of the young ladies came back to the hospital with us in the ambulance car.

? Oct Went to a service in the Y.M.C.A. in the evening. Two solos were rendered.

29th Oct Played Bagatelle in the evening & made a break of 105.

These last three entry dates are on a separate scrap of paper to the list refered to. On the rear is a pencil drawing of a cat at rest made by my father.

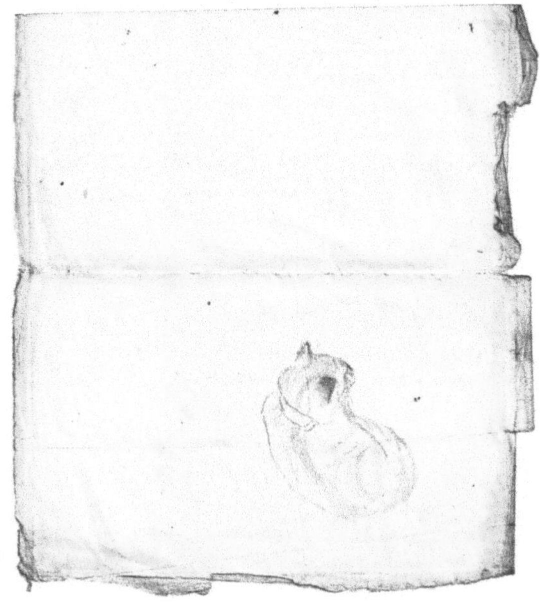

Dec 13th Left the hospital and caught the 9.20pm train for Wptn.[20] Travelled with Ordinaire as far as Crewe where I changed for W'pton.

Dec 14th Arrived home about 7am on the 14th.

Dec 16th Went to Lichfield Road.

20 Wolverhampton.

Dec 20th Ret'd home after calling at Church St.[21]

Dec 22nd Went to Villa Road a[fter] calling at Church St. Slept there the night. (Ditto Villa Road).

Dec 23rd Returned home.

Dec 26th Went to Lichfield Road.[22]

Dec 27th Caught the 4.20pm train for New St. for my journey to Hornsea a[fter] missing the 2.54pm. Changed at Sheffield caught the 8.45pm train for Church Fenton (am Sheff .6.30pm) . Changed again before getting to Hull. Arr. Hull 12.30am 28th.

Dec 28th Caught the 6.40 am train at Hull for Hornsea arriving at the Hutments about 8.30 am.

Dec 29th Had photograph taken.

1918

Jan 5th Left the Hutments & went to Napleton.

Jan 6th Special day of Prayer. Went to Napleton Ch.[23] in the morning & to the Hornsea Wesleyan Ch. in the evening.

Jan 7th Fired first to [two] practices part 3.

Jan 9th Reported sick , M.D. Called for photographs.

Jan 10th Fired remaining four practices part 3.[24]

Jan 11th Returned to Hutments.

21 These two addresses are not explained.

22 With the diaries is an address book in which some of the entries are listed. It is possible that these addresses are entered and may show later who lives at each.

23 Chapel?

24 Contained within the diaries bundle are two practice roundel targets annotated on their reverse as Colchester 2nd August 1917 with all but one of nine shots within the inner ring. See pages 139 and 140.

Jan 26th Left Hornsea on final leave.

There is then a small page with various notes including train times from Birmingham to Hornsea with the changes. Also a sketch. Could it be of the Kaiser?

On the rear of this my father has written a poem:

When The Barrage Lifts – By Ac J. P. Little – Ypres

Do you know an hour in Life's long years
So filled with unspeakable thoughts and fears,
Do you know of a soul who could tell his mind
To another, and consolation find?
And yet, with it all, a marvellous calm
To hearts disquieted – perfect balm –
While the mist of dawn so turgidly drifts
In that hour of hours – when the barrage lifts.
And you – in such an hour have passed
Beyond recalling – Yet at the last,
When the mists of uncertainty melt away
In the dawning light of Eternal day,
We shall meet again in the vast forever
And gain rewards for the Great Endeavour,
When the Tares from the Wheat – the Garnisher siflo;
In that Hour of hours – when the Barrage Lifts.
(Sunday Pictorial 18th Nov. 1917)

The next small scrap of paper in the diaries is also double sided and is reproduced below. On one side there appears to be various notes about train times for his journey to Hornsea with a small sketch and an address for Ordinaire in Jersey, while on the reverse is a poem about the shelling of Ypres. See above.

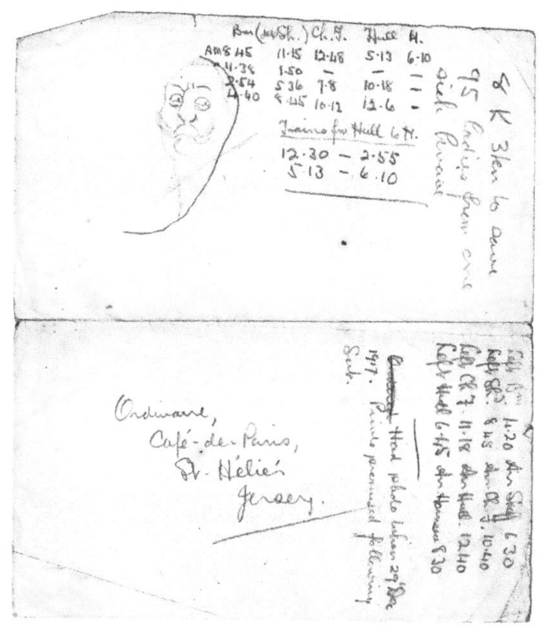

Bm (New St.)	Ch. G.	Hull	H.
AM 8.45	11.15	12.48	5.13	6.10
11.38	1.50	–	–	–
2.54	5.36	7.8	10.18	–
4.40	9.45	10.12	12.6	–

Trains for Hull to H.

12.30 – 2.55
5.13 – 6.10

Ordinaire,
Café-de-Paris,
St. Hélier,
Jersey.

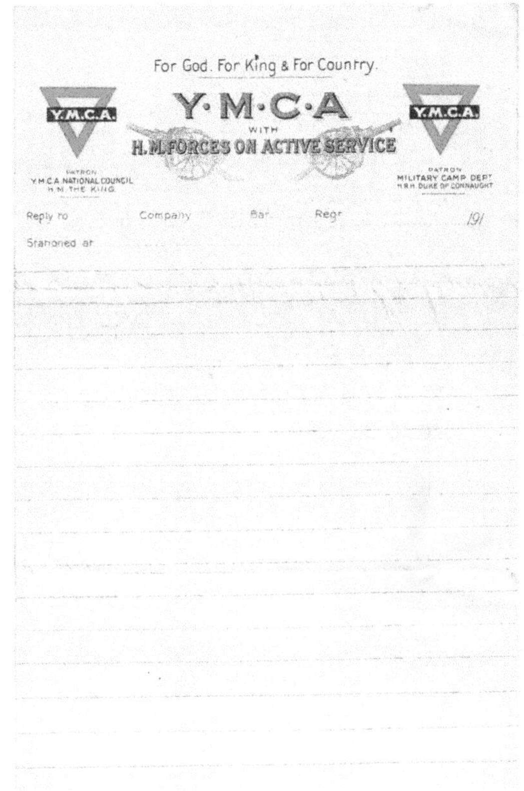

For God. For King & For Country.

Y.M.C.A.

Y·M·C·A

WITH

H.M. FORCES ON ACTIVE SERVICE

Y.M.C.A.

PATRON
Y.M.C.A. NATIONAL COUNCIL
H.M. THE KING

PATRON
MILITARY CAMP DEPT
H.R.H. DUKE OF CONNAUGHT

Reply to .... Company .... Bat. .... Regt 191

Stationed at ....

1917.
Oct. 4th Wounded in Polygon Wood. Removed to clearing station at Poperhinge same day.
" 5th Moved to hosp. at Godewaersvelde.
" 7th Moved from Godewaersvelde
" 8th Arrived at 20th Gen. Hosp. at Camiers.
" 14th } Left Camiers at midnight on the 14th for Calais & sailed
" 15th } from there on the 15th at Dover. Left Dover 4.30 pm.
" 16th Arrived at Merryflats W.H., Govan, Glasgow at 4.30 am.
Dec. 13th Left the hospital & caught the 9.20 pm. train for ~~[illegible]~~ W'pton. Travelled with Ordinaire as far as Crewe where I changed for
14th W'pton. Arrived home about 7 a.m on the 14th.
16th Went to Lichfield Rd.
20th Retd home in calling at Church St.
22nd Went to Villa Road in calling at Church St. slept there the night
23rd Returned home.
26th Went to Lichfield Rd.
27th Caught the 4.20 pm train for New St. for my journey to Hornsea in missing the 2.54 p.m. Changed at Sheffield & caught the 8.45 pm train for Church Fenton. (arr. Sheff. 6.30 pm.) Changed again before getting to Hull. Arr Hull 12.30 am 28th.
28th Caught the 6.40 am. train at Hull for Hornsea arriving at the Hutments about 8.30 am.
1918. 29th Had photograph taken
Jan 5th Left the Hutments & went to Mappleton.
6th Special day of Prayer. Went to Mappleton Ch. in the morning & to the Hornsea Wesleyan Chapel in the evening.
7th Fired first to practices part III.
9th Reported sick, MD.
Called for photographs.
10th Fired remaining four practices part III.
11th Returned to Hutments.
26th Left Hornsea on final leave.

His entries during January 1918 now continue:

Jan 26th. Went home on 6 days draft leave. Travelled via Leeds. Downes went down same time. Played him a game of billiards in the Y.U. at Leeds. Left Hornsea 7.50 am. Left Leeds 12.35 pm . Arrived home about 5.30 pm.

Jan. 27th. Went to Lichd. Rd.[25] Went to Christ Ch. in the evening with Beatie, Mabel & Elsie.

Jan. 28th. Stayed at Lichfield Rd. all day. Gave Elsie, Mabel, Daisy & Beatie a photograph. Called at Church St. in the evening & went home by the 10.25.

Jan. 29th. Went to the pictures in the evening.

Jan. 30th. Doctor called on mother. Gave Idwal[26] telegram to send to Hornsea. Recd. reply same evening granting extension until 5th Feb. Went to pictures in the evening.

Jan. 31st. Went to the pictures in the afternoon & gave Idwal & Blodwen[27] the money to go. Took Myfanwy[28] to the pictures in the evening. Sent ?? to Mrs Hartwell saying I would call on the morrow.

Feb. 1st. Went to Bm. After dinner & on arrival went straight to Villa Road. Stayed the night.[29]

Feb.2nd. Called at Church St. after dinner[30] & returned to Villa Road for tea. Doris took me to the Elite in the evening. Stayed for supper. Mrs. Hartwell gave me box of cigs(5 ogf). Got down to Lichfield Rd. about 10.45pm. Took Mrs. Hunt some tea.

Feb. 3rd. Beatie woke me up & asked me if I was going to chapel. I got up & met Beatie & Elsie by Christ Church about 12.30 & went into Aston Park. Retd. For dinner & went to Christ Ch. with Beatie & Elsie in the evening.

Feb. 4th. Returned to Wn. in the evening after wishing good bye at Lichd. Rd. Mabel & Elsie came to the car[?].

25 Lichfield Road.

26 His younger brother.

27 His younger sister.

28 His youngest sister by 20 years so she would have been only 3 or 4 at this time.

29 This is the address of Doris Hartwell who is listed in an address book along with others he mentions including those above. I return to this book later in the diaries.

30 Church Street is the then home of his sister Miss E.A. Roberts: known as Lizzie.

Feb. 5th. Left home to catch 12.25 for Bm. Father took my kit bag to the station. Did not see Blodwen & Myfanwy before leaving. Missed the 12.25 & caught the 12.45. Arrived at New St. 1.40. Met Mabel & Elsie & caught the 1.50 for Stockport. Gave Mabel ¼ lb of tea. Changed at Stockport for Stalybridge. Caught train there straight through for Hull. Caught 9 o'c train there for Hornsea as having some refreshments.

Feb. 6th. Reported sick & got M.D. S.U. Close put me on draft. Drew an extra tunic, boots, trousers & got an extra shirt & a cap comforter.

There is then a missing eight days.

Feb. 14th. Reported sick. Had hot fermentation put on face 3 times during day & "no duty".

Feb. 15th. Reported sick again & had hot fermentations on three times during the day and was ordered not to go outside the hut. The Doctor came to the hut in the afternoon & examined all the occupants believing, I think, that I had got the mumps.

Feb. 16th. Reported sick again & the Doctor told me to leave the fermentations off & rub my face with Vaseline & he marked me fit for draft. The Sgt. Major sent for me about 2.30 in the afternoon & told me I was to go with the draft that afternoon and I got everything ready& left the Hutments about 4.20. We marched down to Hornsea station & left there about 5.15. We changed at Hull & Doncaster & again when we got to London. Just before we got to Potters Bar Station the lights in the train went out as a raid (I assume was taking place) & during the time the train was in darkness two of the draft ??? (Cun, Can, Cern) & someone else got away leaving all their guns labelled in the carriage. When we got to Kings Cross station all the drafts lined up, about 20 having hopped it, and we marched through London to Charing Cross Station where we got into the train for Folkestone.

End of Recuperation

Feb. 17th. It was about 2am when we started from Charing Cross & Reveille was being sounded as we marched into the billets at Folkestone at 6 o'clock in the morning. We had a good breakfast & a good dinner &

some rations to take with us on the boat. I sent a few letters off from the Y.M. We crossed over about 4.30 in the afternoon on a very calm sea. It was an ordinary troop ship but a great deal too cold on deck so Lt. Daly & I went below deck & lay on the wet floor in the troop-room until we were near Boulogne. It was dark when we got there & the "Star of Antwerp" was unloading passengers (Generals & c) when we steamed up aside of her & we had to cross her deck to get on shore. We had a difficulty in finding the Durhams on the square but we found them eventually & then marched off to ST. Martins Camp, where I went on my previous visit to France, & slept there the night under canvas.

Feb. 18th. Reveille was at 5.30 in the morning but I'd had a good night's sleep & felt quite refreshed. We had three blankets each & as three of us slept together we manag(ed) to make ourselves quite warm & very comfortable under the circo.[31] Breakfast in the morning consisted of cold bacon, bread & some tea. We marched off at 8 o'clock and after about half an hour's marching reached the motor transports which carried us to Etaples. It was 9.15 am when we started off in the cars & 11.40 when we reached the camp now known as "E. Depot". We had a kit inspection before dinner & with the Waacs in charge of the dining room, things were very clean all the way round, very much better than they were in August last. Wrote letters in the Scottish Hut in the evening. Slept under canvas but it was rather cold.

Feb. 19th.

Reveille at 5 o'clock for the boys because they were on station piquet but I was reporting sick & didn't get up until about 6.15. When I saw the doctor he marked me for the marque & I got into bed there about 10.30. He placed me in there on account of my swollen face but pains in the back & a bad headache troubled me a great deal more & my temperature was over 102 by night.

Feb 20th.

I saw the Doctor again about 9 o'c in the morning & he ordered me for hospital. I was taken down to the 24th General in the morning and went to bed in No 27A Ward & No 5 bed.

31 Circumstances?

Feb 21st.

I feel a lot better but my head seems heavy & the pains still trouble me in the back and in the abdomen. Wrote several letters in the evening.

Feb 22nd.

A Doctor interviewed me in the morning & I told him about the pains in the small of the back. Read two books during the day.

Feb 23rd.

Still complained of the pains to the Doctor. He said I could get up that day. Did not get up & the Sister enquired the reason why & I told her that I hadn't got the togs.

Feb 24th(Sund).

Read "The Lost World" by A Conan Doyle. Very interesting. Rec'd cigarette issue, 4 packs of "Trumpeters".

Feb 25th.

Read "The Little Hour of Peter Wells" by ...[32] Got up at dinner. Went to bed again soon after tea.

Feb 26th.

Read "Thalassa!" by Mrs Baillie Reynolds. Got up for a little after dinner.

Feb 27th.

Got up about 10 o'c.

Feb 28th.

Bailed out.

Mar 1st.

Rotten weather. Paraded before Colonel at 8.30 & marked C.C. & (Rest in Camp).

32 My father doesn't say by whom but I have established that it was written by David Whitelaw and published in 1913. In 1921 it became a silent film produced in the Netherlands and directed by Maurits Binger & B.E. Doxat-Pratt, with the screenplay co-written by David Whitelaw and Eliot Stannard.

Mar 2nd.

Drew togs from pack store at 9 am. Paraded at 1.30 pm & marched to "Con" Camp. Paraded before Doctor after tea & he marked me Convalescant [his spelling]. Slept in Bell Tent, boards & pallia's & blankets. Spent evening in Y.M.C.A. (No 6 Convalescent Go. Naples)[33]

Mar 3rd.

Went to Non-c service in Y.M.C.A. in the morning. Went to Bible Class at 2.30: subject – "The wrong & the right uses of the Bible"

There is then a gap in the diaries up to: –

Mar 11th.(Sunday)

Read "The Bronze Eagle" by Baroness Orczy. Dancing in the morning.[34]

Mar 16th.

Went to Trouville in the morning & had dancing on the beach.[35]

On the rear of the last entry sheet are the following notes:–

Mar 17th.

On Engineers' fatigue in the morning taking down barbed wire round Fritz' (prisoners of war) camp. Went to town for dinner. Walked round

33 Or is it Maples?

34 Does he mean 'dancing'?

35 Does he mean 'dancing'?

the Town & along the beach then had tea & biscuits at the Y.M.C.A. Went to "Tommie & Sammies" Restaurant & had tea, bread, eggs & chips (2 frs). Finished up at the ????? [blank here] after a very pleasant time.

Mar 18th.(Mon)

Danc'g on the field in the morning. Went to see No.2 Camp Concert Party at Deauville Casino in the a'rnoon & had pass for Trouville for the evening. Concert very good especially "The Humming Birds". Sketch after Fred Karno. Had a cup of tea & biscuits at the Y.M. in town & then went for a walk round. Went to "Tommy & Sammies" Restaurant & had a tea of eggs & chips & bread(1fr 60c). Finished up at the ?????[blank again].

Mar 19th. (Tues).

M.O. parade 9.30. Played footer at 11.30. Beat K Coy 2-0. Watched boxing after dinner. Also dancing before tea. "Ribbon Dance", "Yorkshire Sword Dance", "Maurice[I think] Jink", "Lancashire Old Barn Dance", "Princess Royal Dance" &C. Very good concert by Lena Ashwell's Concert Party in the evening.

Mar 20th.(Wed).

Dancing in Y.M.C.A. in the morning. Watched boxing in the afternoon. Watched football & rugby after tea & went to Service at S.C.A. in the evening.

The following entries were written on letter note paper headed The Salvation Army whilst in Trouville between 21st and 31st March 1918.

Mar 21st (Thurs)

Dancing on field in the morning. Lost spoon in dining hall – dinner time. Wrote a long letter to Mabel in the afternoon. Went to the Salvation Army Hut in the evening & heard Commissioner Higgins. Miss Mary Bramwell Booth was there also & read a letter rec'd from her father & addressed to the boys. The hall was packed & men were standing on ladders outside the windows. The service, like the usual Salvation Army services, was very emotional. Had a very pretty sing-song in hut until 11pm.

Mar 22nd.(Friday)

Gardening in the morning. Went to hear Lena Ashwell's Concert Party in the Y.M.C.A. in the afternoon. Nearly had my ribs broken in the crush going in. Artistes included mezzo soprano, contralto, violinist, hand bells & eloqutionist [his spelling] who recited Kipling's "If" & Kipling's "Thousandth Man".

Mar 23rd (Saturday)

Gardening in the morning until 11 o'clock. Had a game of Solo before dinner & again after dinner. Read "Laddie" by Gene Stratton Porter in the afternoon. Washed a towel. Flemming (R.Fs) lent me a franc. Had supper in dining hall. Went to S.C.A. in the evening & wrote home. Many men got up during the service to testify their love for Jesus & amongst them was a nigger from Jamaica. Had a very lively sing-song in the hut in the evening. On first piquet.

Mar 24th(Sunday)

Paraded for M.O.'s inspection in the morning. Owing to "Jerry's" big push a lot of men were marked out but owing to a bad cold I was marked "B". Wrote letters in the afternoon. Went to the S.C.A. service in the evening. At 10.30 pm the Sgt. Major called us out owing to an air raid & we stood outside the orderly room for an hour before we were dismissed. "E" Coy was called out by mistake as "F" Coy were on fire piquet.

Mar25th(Mon)

A big evacuation took place today. I was on duty in the dining hall for the day. Had a game of billiards with Flemming in the afternoon. Wrote letters at the S.C.A. in the evening & stayed for the service.

Mar 26th(Tues)

Inspection of camp by C.O. in the morning. I was given a permanent job in the Dining Hall. Another big evacuation today. Flemming went on it. Went to the S.C.A. service in the evening . Moved to No. 1U hut.

Mar 27th(Wed)

At the dining hall until about 7 o'clock in the evening. Large convoy arrived straight from the line. Fag issue(3pcts).

Mar 28th(Thursday)

At the dining hall until about 10 pm owing to a convoy of wounded from around St. Quentin. Had a pass in but couldn't go to town. Pay-day (10 francs).

Mar 29th(Good Friday)

At the dining until after tea time. Went to the service at the S.C.A. hut in the evening.

Mar 30th(Sat)

At the dining hall until tea time. Had a pass and went to Trouville in the evening. Did not meet any of the boys in town. Helped in the dining hall when I got back until about 10.15 pm. Another convoy had come in (over 1500).

Mar 31st (Easter Sunday)

At the dining hall all day. Another convoy came in. About 1000.

The following entries were also written on letter note paper headed The Salvation Army whilst in Trouville between 1st April and 6th April 1918.

April 1st(Mon)

Medical inspection in the morning. I was marked fit. In the dining hall until tea time. Had a pass and went to Trouville in the evening. Did not meet any of the lads. Had supper in the Y.M.C.A.

April 2nd(Tues)

At the dining hall all day. Tried to get my great-coat exchanged for a new one but no luck. Wrote letters in the Y.M.C.A. in the evening.

April 3rd(Wed)

In the dining hall all day.

April 4th(Thursday)

In the dining hall first thing. Medical inspection at 10.30. I was marked A so I finished in the dining hall. Had a pass for the evening and went to Trouville with Lambert of the 2/8 Manchesters. Walked about the town and the beach until 6 O'clock & then went into the Hotel Bourgogne until 8 o'clock. Supped 3 bottles of Malaga & 1 Bottle of Port between us. A gentleman treated the Tommies who were in there to two glasses of beer each. Lambert and I were carried home paralytic drunk and I knew nothing until I awoke about 4 am next morning.

April 5th(Friday)

My clothes were in such a state that I had to get my working suit changed for a new rig-out which I managed to do as I had not signed for the working suit. The evacuation party had tea at 2.30 & we left the camp after being dished out with rations about 4.45. No.13 Con[?] Camp travelled in cattle trucks. The scenery was very pretty all the way to Rouen. We passed, on the way up to Rouen, through Touques, Pont L'Eveque, Tierville-les-Parcs, Legrand Jardin, Lisieux & numerous other stations but I was asleep part of the time so I could not make a note of them. We had quite a long stop at Lisieux and during that time chaps were selling their kit; shirts 2fr, pants 2fr, socks 1fr, & other articles went at ridiculously low prices. Parcels and boxes were stolen from the platform & the contents sold when we reached Rouen.

April 6th(Saturday)

Arrived at Rouen about 7.30 am & were marched to the Rest Camp on the Quai. I had some refreshments at the canteen while there & met 2[J,I?].U.S. Smith of the 15th D.L.I. A lot of gambling went on on the river side and from one of the numerous stalls. I bought a souvenir ring(1fr 50c). I had made friends with a young chap named Dillon of the Liverpool Scottish (came from Matlock) while there and we travelled the rest of our journey to Etaples together. We paraded at 1.30 pm for moving off & my friend and I nearly missed the party through watching the pranks of a little French kiddie on one of the boats on the river. A piece of rope was stretched from one end of the boat to the other and a little kiddie was tied by another small piece of rope around the waist & the rope being attached to the long piece of rope by an iron ring the kiddie could walk about from one end to the other. We travelled down from Rouen in ordinary French carriages but I was not half so comfortable in them as I was in the truck going up to Rouen. The scenery as seen from the carriage window on leaving Rouen station for Etaples was simply superb. The train stopped on the bridge over the river Seine and I saw one of the finest sights that I have ever seen. Rouen Cathedral being close to the railway bridge shows up clearly and the river being covered with boats, tugs, motolaunches ??the whole made a very beautiful picture. There are two railway bridges and the one between us and the cathedral had 8 huge spans. Some building was going on the other end of the bridge & huge wooden pillars[piles] were being driven into the earth by a steam hammer arrangement. For quite a long way down the line from Rouen were scores of little kiddies shouting "Bisceet" (bis(care)t) &" Bully Beuf". I dropped off to sleep, when it got dark, in the lavatory, & woke up at 2am the train having stopped. I got out to see where we were & it turned out that we were at Etaples. I didn't stay out long but turned in again and had a nap until about 6am.

April 7th(Sunday)

We got out of the train at Etaples station about 6am & were marched down to No.9 Rest Camp. We had some breakfast & then a medical inspection. I reported that I did not feel well so was sent to Medical Board Depot to have my temperature taken twice a day. Dillon & a Durham who had travelled all the way from Trouville with [us?] were recommended for a board. I went into the town of Etaples with them in the evening.

April 8th(Mon)

Still at the U.B. depot. No fatigue. Went to the town of Etaples in the evening. Dillon & Durham marked Active % returned to their I.B.Do.[36]

April 9th(Tues)

Saw the doctor in the morning & he recommended me for a board. Went to town again in the evening.

April 10th(Wed)

Went before medical board & got marked Active. Returned to Depot at 1.30. Met Stafford of the 2/7 in the evening& he & I went to the N.Z's canteen. He treated me to a franc supper of eggs & spuds. Watched the Nancs[?] after that.

April 11th(Thurs)

Drew full kit in the morning. Inspected by C.O. & later by M.O. Went down to the Bull Ring in the afternoon for gassing. Went to the Canadian Y.M.C.A. in the evening with Stafford & played him [at] billiards for an hour. He sd[said?] that Squires had gone to the 16th London Reg

36 Could stand for Infantry Battalion ditto or International/Internal Base Depot.

about a fortnight since. Changed my quarters in the evening & went to K. Lines. Reported sick in the evening.

April 12th(Fri)

Attended M.O. & he put me down for marquee. Handed my equipment , rifle & bayonet, water proof sheet, steel helmet & respirator in to the stores & went to the marquee about 11 am. Had a quiet day in there and felt quite alright except for pains in the back.

April 13th(Saturday)

Saw the M.O. in the morning and was marked out of the marquee. Drew equipment & rifle etc. Drew 10 frs pay at 10.30 am. Went through the gas at the Bull Ring in the afternoon for another respirator. A draft came in at night about 10pm from the 2/7 at Colchester & Dennis Horseman was with them Went to the town in the evening with Stafford & had some beer & stout. Had supper at the N.Z. hut. I treated.

April 14th(Sunday)

Met Dennis & we talked & talked. Went on Church Parade in the morning. When "God Save The King" was sung only about 6 men in the whole gathering of about 3000 sung. One man with a baritone voice seemed to be singing a solo in the rear of the building. I was warned for draft when I got back to depot. At two o'clock I was told that I should be leaving Etaples at 3.30 pm. I had tea about 3 o'clock, drew iron rations and ammunition but I moved off with the party at 5.30pm after wishing Dennis & Stafford the best of luck etc. I bought some bread & tea etc. from the Y.M.C.A. on the siding. I was the only member of the draft for the 8th D.L.I. & carried my own papers with parlars[? particulars?]. I got into a truck with N.Fs[Northumberland Fusiliers?] of the 50th Divn. & some M.Gs[machine gunners?]. We had a fire in the truck but I got no sleep.

April 15th(Monday)

We got out of the truck at Berguelle about 3am & went into the Y.M.(which had been evacuated) as we thought for a night's kip, but just as we settled down we had to get out to make room for some refuges (lunatics from a hospital) from a town that Jerry was shelling. The same thing happened when I had lain down in the waiting room on the station platform, so I had no sleep during the whole of the night. The refuges were taken away in a train eventually so we hung about in the Y.M. until about 11 o'clock when the 50th Divn. Lads moved off for Air. Started marching with full pack about 11am. Marched through Mametz to a village three ks beyond Air.The latter place was a little the worse for Fritz's bombing. There were ten of us in the party including an S.M. We got a lift in a transport about half-way between Berguelle & Air as far as the station at the latter place. We arrived at the Reinforcement Camp at 1.15pm thoroughly tired out. I warmed some tea which I had in my water bottle & with a little bread & bully beef managed to enjoy a dinner. We drew some tea & sugar from the stores for tea-time but could get no rations & had to be content with our iron rations. We drew rations for the morrow (no bread) about 7.30pm. I had a well-earned sleep that night in a cow shed on a farm.

April 16th(Tuesday)

Got up about 8 o'clock & had a good breakfast of fried bacon & biscuits & tea. Were told to clean up and get ready to move at 9.30 am (50th Division men only). Had dinner of Malionocis[?] & hard biscuits about 11 o'clock. Did not leave Mathes but had another good night's sleep.

April 17th(Wednesday)

Ordered to get marching order ready for first thing after breakfast & fall in for moving off. Left Mathes about 11 am and after a long march passing through Air we arrived at the 151st Brigade's Hdqts., tired out about 2.30 pm. I went to "C" Company's Billets of the 8th D.L.I. on the far side of the canal at Willes. I got some hard biscuits fm the Sgt. Major for tea rations.

April 18th(Thursday)

Had a good breakfast. Felt very sick after dinner. Received ten francs pay after tea. I did not have any tea as I was too sick. Lay down for the night about 5 pm. Warned for Battn. Hdqrs. Guard for the following night. Was very sick during the night.

April 19th(Friday)

Did not have any bfst. as I was too sick. Reported sick but I did not see the Doctor. Borrowed some web equipment & cleaned up for guard. Did not have any dinner. Tried a little tea but was very sick after it. Mounted guard at 5 pm. Came back to billet for great coats. Got Kirkup's and my own. Brigadier came round while I was sentry & asked why I did not turn out the guard. I told him I understood retreat had gone. He looked at his watch & sd that that was so. Very cold in the tent & I had a rotten night.

April 20th(Saturday)

Had a good breakfast of ham & two eggs & some tea & bread & butter. Hdqrs cook cooked it but we did not get it until after ten o'clock. I felt quite sick again after eating. No dinner rations were sent down so we had to buy what we could get from the farm house. I had two fried eggs & some French bread & I made some tea with some spare tea & sugar which I had. We were relieved at 5 o'clock. We fell in for inspection without respirators & the officer would not let us go for them so we had to return later in the evening for the respirators and coats.

April 21st(Sunday)

[This is my father's 24th birthday]

Went on C. of E. parade in the morning. Had a sleep in the afternoon. Felt sick again today. Went to Air in the evening & called at the B.E. Canteen for cigs & then had some tea in the Y.M.C.A. Went to the service in the concert room held by the Rev. Moore MA of M'chester at 6.30. Had a violent fit of coughing while in there & was glad when the service ended. Got back to billet about 9.15 feeling quite bad. Was coughing & vomiting during the night.

[He makes no mention that it is his birthday but this is not surprising given his state of health].

April 22nd(Monday)

Reported sick & went to see the doctor. I explained to him what was the matter with me & he gave me some castor oil & marked the sick report Diarrhoe'a & med. & duty. Went down to the stores with the Quarter & carried some small kit back to billets.

April 23rd, 24th & 25th.

Nothing much done. I went down to Air once or twice but there was nothing to be got down there. We had a bath & a clean change in Air during our stay.

April 26th.

Reveille at 2.30am, bfat 3.0am, fall-in at 4.0am. Marched down to the main Road & boarded the buses. Arrived at a station just beyond Lillers about 11.30am. Entrained in horse boxes about tea time. Travelled all night.

27th April.

Passed through Rouen & went round Paris but did not pass through the station. Arrived at our destination about 6.30am on the...

28th April.

Marched about 6 kils. to our billets at Arcis le Pousart.

29&30 & May 1st,2nd,3rd &4th.

Parades in the mornings but very little doing in the afternoons. We had a bath whilst here but no clean change. We had one field day when the Division turned out for the General's inspection. I was appointed Scout & Sniper on the 2nd.

May 5th.

Left Arcis le Pousart about 5.30am & passing through Fismes arrived at Brislieux, a distance of about 18 kils., thoroughly tired out. Slept the night in French billets.

May 6th.

Bought some eggs for myself & the Sgt Major. Had hot supper, tea & rissoles at 10.30pm. Fell in at 12 o'clock in full marching order & marched off. Very tiring march & raining.

May 7th.

Arrived at destination in reserve lines about 4 miles behind lines. Comfy billets, wire netting beds.

May 8,9,10,11&12.

Very quiet time excepting one evening when Johnny sent two or three whizz bangs over. I was fetching some cheese fm Co. /q. when a shell hit the Church about 4 yds away from me. Lectures on observation by Lt. Harrison in the mornings. No canteen so we had to manage without cigs & c.

Rations fairly good.

May 13th.

Left Chauderdes about 10.30pm & arrived at the trenches (Trenchee Saussien) in Supports about 1am on the 14th.

May 14th.

I went on for the first hour gas sentry.

May 15,16,17&18.

Rations, water, ammunition & trench boards were carried to the front line at night -time. I did a little observing one morning. Gas sentries were posted night & day. Fritz bombarded the dumps heavily on the night of the 18th.

May 19th.

Left the support trenches & went up to the front line on the Craonne Plateau. I was standing to on No.3 Post, 10 Platoon with L/C T. P. Nicholson, Pvts. Page, Wood & Barbour. We had to take cover from machine guns several times.

May 20th.

Stood down about 4.30 am. Had breakfast & then I slept until dinner time about 1 o'clock. L/C Nicholson spoke to Capt. Williams & then I was put on observing in the O.P. Transferred my quarters to C.H.Q.

There follows a selection of pages from a small note book illustrating a continuation of his diaries together with entries for friends and comrades. [They have been sorted out of order by scanning].

Out of date order is a note at the top of the page for 1918 headed "Pay" which I believe relates to his repatriation following Polygon Wood. It reads:- Sailed across on Oct 15/17 in the Pietre de Corringle.

Another note [very feint] at the top of the page with a circular mark half way down reads:-

Leaving Trouville-Deauville (5.45....) Tourques-Port-Leveque-Fierville les Pares-Legrand Jardin-LisieuRouen(April 5,6&7 1918)

He then describes a tank under which is another note:-

These entries are out of date order but have been included as written . The continuity is only interrupted by a short reference to October 1917 and Polygon Wood, the remaining text is sequential.

26,27 April 1918 Left Willes in [then the mark hides the next word but I think it is "buses"] at 6.30am. Left stn. Near Lillers 4.30am. Left Rouen 2pm(27th).

On the next but one page is a list of names which I interpret are of those with whom he fought on the front line at The Battle of The Aisne on 27th May 1918. They seem to read as follows:-

L/C Dodds reported missing Sesuine do.
Pve Salmon do do
C L/C Stagg. Wounded & prisoner.
C Sig. Ashdale. " "
C Pve. Cunningham " "
C Lt. Ass. Ajut. Prisoner.
C Orderley Room Srgt. "
C Sgt. Cook. "
C L/C Cook. "
C Watson, Cook. "
C Sgt. Kirkup, wounded.
C Crawshaw. do.
Sgt. Wraith, (D. Comp), wounded & prisoner.
Drummer Thorpe4" Yorks Com. Wounded in R leg, died of (q. bue?) lock jaw.
C Pvte. Meeking ; sweet shop, Snow Hill.[37] Prisoner, wounded.
C.S.M. Brown; wounded & prisoner.

There then follows a four line sentence only 11mm deep but with striking meaning.

Capt. Williams, Capt Wilkinson,[38] L/c Tof brown, Dick Saunders, Mickey Menham, Jack Hunt, Sig. Ashdale, 2 o[ther] signallers & myself

37 I think that this refers to the railway station in Birmingham.

38 The diary of Captain Henry Wilkinson has been published in detail and accounts from the day before the onslaught 26th May to 30th December 1918 under the title From Craonne to Hull.

fought to the last on the railway embankment on the morning of the 27/5/18 & Sgt. Farley wounded.

Below are images of that railway embankment in June 2017.

The route of the old rail line towards Craonne station

Another view of the embankment

The line leaves the wood heading for Craonne station

The Old Rail Bed leading into the Bois de Beau Marais

The overgrown embankment

More Images of the Railway Embankment Area: Spring 2019.

Site of the former track bed [Ouvrage du Chemin de Fer] where C Coy, 8 DLI made a stand viewed from the German attack location. This is the region of C Coy HQ with Battalion HQ further back.

View from the C Coy, 8 DLI defence area looking towards the German attack position.

View from a German attack point on the railway line heading towards the embankment.

View from the area of Armingdon Trench which was further back heading towards the embankment. The Germans at this point had penetrated the front line defences. La Corne Redoubt would be to the right on the edge of the trees.

This shows the British view from the railway line to the front line which is in the trees. This image is 100 yards in front of the embankment where my father "fought to the last". In the front line B Coy were in the trees to the right and D Coy at front right at Chevreux: they were wiped out in the barrage and initial assault. The track was the railway line and this is the route which it is thought my father probably took in his first moments as a POW.

Map of the Area

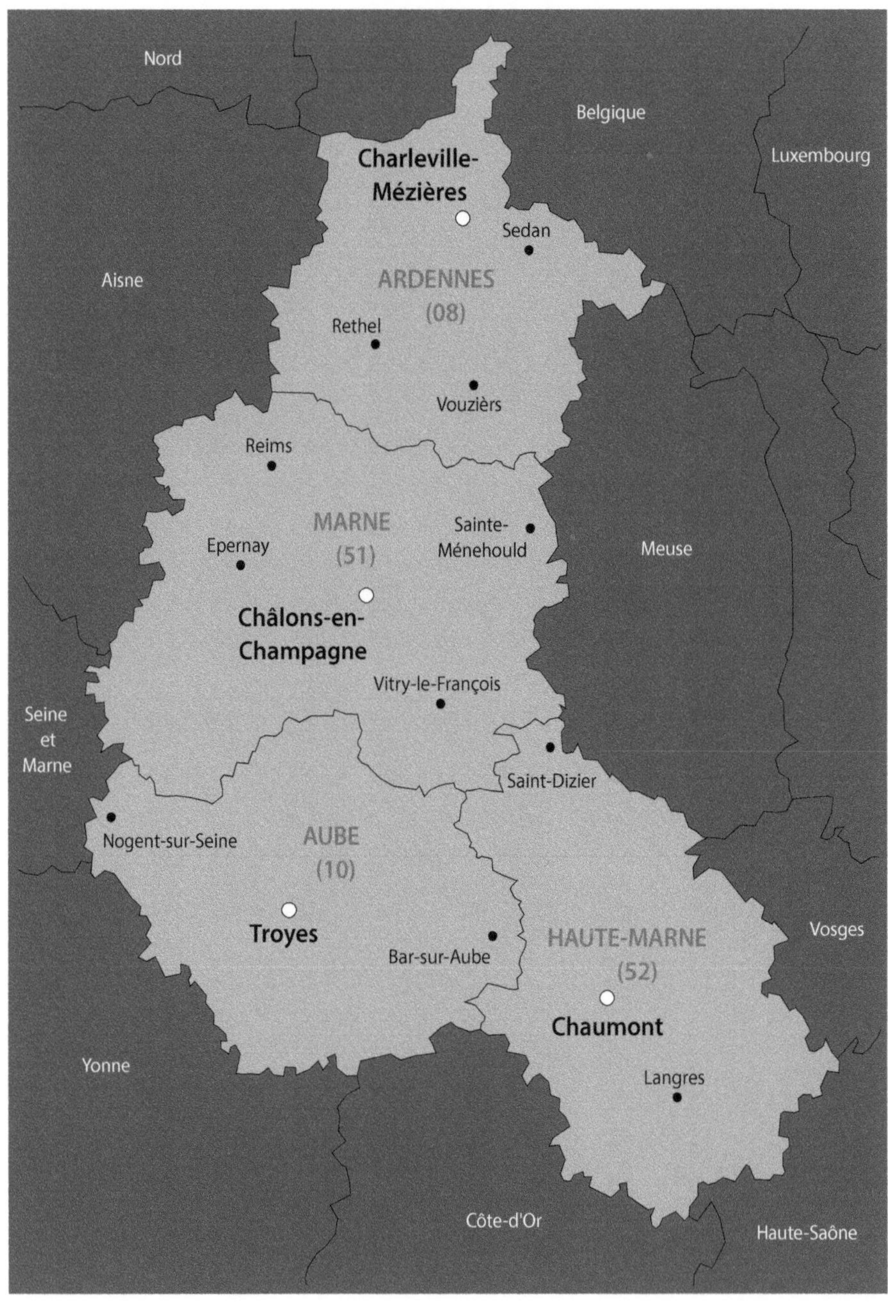

Continuing from the notebook the next page but one begins:–

1918

May 27th. M Barrage at 1AM. Advance 4AM. Took message to Capt. Williams frm Lt. Wilson 5.30am. Wounded about 6.30am. carried to Corbeny & stayed there part of the night, then removed in motor to train & taken to clearing station at..................

[There were only two clearing stations in this area: numbers 37 and 48, the nearest of which was number 37. Fred Ashmore, from whose help and assistance I have benefited during this project, has written much about the Battle of The Aisne and had two relatives also wounded on this day whilst serving in the 6th Battalion of the DLI when my father was in 8th DLI. They were taken to CCS37 so must have been there with private Roberts after also having been on the front line with him. Fred has a shell casing which he found in the summer of 2018 on the same railway embankment referred to in my father's diary which he believes contained shrapnel. My father's injuries on The Aisne were from shrapnel. My father was taken POW on 28 May.]

28th. Tu. Treated very well at this place but wounds still undressed.

29th. W. Allies aeroplanes bombed the place & just missed hitting the marquee.

30th. Th. Still at the clearing station.

31st. Fr. Moved from there by train to a hospital. Had better food on train & a very comfortable bed.

June 1st. Sat. Arrived at Limburg in Lorraine & taken to Labry hospital. A very dirty place it seemed at first. Had wounds dressed for first time in the afternoon. Food very course. The young nurse treated us all like a lady.

2nd. Su. Food better today. Given a Prisoners Card which I filled in & addressed home.

3rd. M With nothing to do & nothing to read time hangs on terribly. I find in[t] difficult to sleep because of pains in my leg. The shrapnel being left in I think causes more pain.

4th. Tu. The weather still continues to be nice. My leg still pains me. The swelling which rose on 27th has not yet gone down. The head Doctor came round in the evening. My leg was evidently alright.

5th. W. Leg still pains. Thorpe very bad & revd[received?] injections in the leg & arms. 4 altogether. Taken into another ward for the night. I had my bed moved up to where Thorpe used to be next to Sgt. Wraith.

6th Th. My temp. up to 38.4 in the eveng. I felt very feverish & had a nasty headache. The Doctor ordered for me to have an inoculation. I had it in the evening.

7th. F. Felt very bad again in the morn'g hav'g had no sleep during the night. Temp. 38.8 in the morning. Had my leg dressed in the afternoon. Temp. 38.2 in the even'g. Thorpe very much worse & died in the ward during the night. He being next to me I did not get much sleep until he fell into a peaceful sleep just before he died. He was a Drummer in the 4th E. Yorks & died of Lock-jaw.

8th. St. My temp. was down to Normal, 36.8 in the morn'g & 37.3 in the even'g. I felt better but a little stiff about the neck. I was booked to go to Germany with the next evacuation. My leg still painful.

9th. Su. Leg a little better. The Sgt. came in in the morn'g & wanted my haversack with all my things in from the locker. A General was coming to visit & they were tidying up. I was tak'g the things out but he came towards me with a rush & put them back again. He took the haversack away.

10th. M. The General came round in the morn'g. He did not look very striking. The Sgt. Brought my haversack back in the afternoon & nothing was missing.

11,12,13,14,15,16,17&18. Nothing of importance to report. I had my leg dressed on the 12th. My temperature went up to 39.5 on the 16th (37 normal). Our airmen came over once or twice & dropped bombs quite close to the hospital, once in the daytime.

19th. W. Had my leg dressed in the morn'g. Both Doctors tried to straighten the leg but it was very stiff. I was told to try and walk on it & try & get it straight.

20th. Th. Names taken for moving to another hospital. I was one & had an over-coat (in place of my tunic) & my old trousers issued out to me.

21st. F. The Sgt. Came round & woke us up at 4am. We left the hospital in + motors about 6am & arrived at a hospital near the station where we had coffee & bread & jam. We boarded the hospital train from there & the train started off about 9.30am. The d was very good on the train. The scenery was grand especially in Wur Hemberg just before Mettingen.

22nd. Sa. The food was very good and plentiful. I had a good night's sleep. I did not feel well today. The nurse gave me some sweetened coffee for tea & some sago for supper because my appetite was bad. My temperature was 39.4 in the evening.

23rd. Su. Felt better afr. a good night's sleep. Passed through Ulm in the morning & saw the highest Church in the world(161 metres). Arrived at the hospital about 11.30am & had a bath & a clean shirt & dressing & went to bed. Issued with socks & other necessities. Had soup & fried macaroni & jam for dinner & some hot cocoa afterwards. The cocoa was from the boys of the camp. Had fried macaroni again for supper but no jam.

Entry Record for Limberg.

[The date seems to be later than his actual arrival on 1st June 1918. Also, he records leaving Limberg on 21st June and arriving at Lager Lechfeld on 23rd June 1918.]

FICHE 23 JUIL 1918 P.A. COPIE

1 Lfd. Nr.	2 a) Familienname b) Vorname (nur der Rufname) c) nur bei Russen Vorname des Vaters	3 Dienstgrad	4 a) b) Truppenteil c) Komp.	5 a) b) Gefangennahme (Ort und Tag) c) vorhergehender Aufenthaltsort	6 a) Geburtstag und -Ort b) c) Adresse des nächsten Verwandten
43	[illegible] JOhn [illegible] 13081.	Sergt	A. YORKS. [illegible]	27/5/18 Craonne FrOnt	[illegible] Mrs [illegible] [illegible] Terrace DUrham City.
44	[illegible] [illegible] 92284	[illegible]	R.F.A. 250 Bde. D.	27/5/18 [illegible] FrOnt.	[illegible] Mrs Ellen [illegible] 51 [illegible] Terrace. [illegible]
45	[illegible] Leonard 201122	Sergt Major	1/4. E. YORKS C.	27/5/18 Craonne FrOnt	[illegible] Mrs [illegible] [illegible] Road HULL.
46	OWEN [illegible] [illegible]	[illegible]	1/6. [illegible] Inf 2.	27/5/18 Craonne FrOnt	[illegible] Mrs. Evan OWEN [illegible] [illegible] Anglesly [illegible]
47.	[illegible] Frederick 200145	CORP.	4 YORKS.	27/5/18 Craonne. FrOnt	[illegible] Mrs. [illegible] [illegible] Road RichmOnd.
48.	[illegible] GeOrge. 241732	SOLd.	4. YORKS.	27/5/18 CraOnne FrOnt	14/5/[illegible] [illegible] Mr. [illegible] [illegible] Nursery. [illegible] GrOsmOnt
49	[illegible] Victor.	Lieut.	YORKS	27/5/18 Craonne FrOnt	[illegible] St GeOrges ROad. Brankling Isle Of Wight. (HamptOn [illegible])
50.	[illegible] [illegible] Edwin 235648	CORP.	4. YORKS. W	27/5/18 [illegible] FrOnt	[illegible] [illegible] Mr [illegible] [illegible] ROad. WaltasstOw. [illegible]
51.	RICHARDSON. Harry JOhn. 200132.	SOLD.	RFA. 251.Bde.	27/5/18 CraOnne. FrOnt	[illegible] Mrs RichardsOn. [illegible] Fulham. LONDON [illegible]
52	[illegible] GeOrge.	Lieut.	5 Durham L Inf	27/5/18 CraOnne. [illegible]	17/4/[illegible] TOW LAW Mrs [illegible] Castle TOW LAW. [illegible] Durham.
53	ROBERTS. William JOhn 276410.	SOLD.	8 D L Inf	27/5/18 CraOnne. FrOnt	21/4/94. Llangefni Mrs. ROberts. 145 JOhnsOn Street Blakenall. WOlverhamptOn.

I include here the entry record for Lager Lechfeld, although it is dated 22nd February 1919 by which time he was on his way back to England.

1 Lfd. Nr.	2 a) Familienname b) Vorname (nur der Rufname) c) nur bei Russen Vorname des Vaters	3 Dienstgrad	4 a) b) Truppenteil c) Komp.	5	6 Bemerkungen
137	Kelly, Michael [illegible] 34[illegible]1.	do.	3. York	27. 1[illegible]. 9[illegible]. Liverpool. Mr. E. Kelly, Grosvenor-Rd. Wavertree-Liverpool.	Craonne. 27. 5. 18. Operationsgeb.
138	Kettle, Cl[illegible] 3478[illegible].	do.	do.	1[illegible]. . 99. Bourne. Mrs. L. Kettle, Willin-House Eastgate-Bourne.	do. do. do.
139	Lucas, Robert [illegible]	do.	4 do.	[illegible]. 11. 89. Birmingham. Mrs. A. Lucas, 499 Anl[illegible]tv-Rd. Hull-Yorkshire.	do. do. do.
14[illegible]	Mc. Grath, Mich. 351166.	do.	7 D.L.I.	1[illegible]. 11. [illegible]. Liverpool. Mr. Mc. Grath, 4[illegible] Litchfield-Str. Liverpool.	La-Hutte. do. do.
141	[illegible], Josef [illegible]	do.	R.A.M.C.	4. 3. 98. [illegible] Mr. C. M[illegible], Southview Prudhoe-on-Tyne.	Fismes. do. do.
142	Munro, [illegible] [illegible]27.	L. C.	[illegible]	2[illegible]. 6. 97. Britch-Nir[illegible]. Mrs. Munro, J. [illegible]-Lodge. Crieff-Pertshire.	Craonne. do. do.
143	Metcalfe, [illegible] 43740.	do.	4 Yorks.	7. 7. 98. Thirsk. Mrs. E. Metcalfe, 5[illegible] Poplar-Str. Poppleton-Rd. York.	do. do. do.
144	Owen, [illegible] 91744.	do.	1/6 [illegible]	24. 3. 96. Anglisey Mrs. E. Owen, Bryn-HyFryed, [illegible]-North-Wales.	Gou[illegible]-B[illegible]rney do. do.
145	Roberts, Will. 278410.	do.	9; Durh.	21. 4. 94. Wolverhampton. Mr. Roberts, 45 Johnson-Str. Blakenhall-Wolverhampton	Craonne. do. do.
146	S[illegible]en, Will. 54361.	do.	4; N. Fus.	8. 3. 99. Bridlington. Mr. S[illegible]en, 15 Nelson-Str. Bridlington.	do. do. do.
147	Sencir, Will. 23367.	do.	5. York.	12. 6. 80. Grimesthorpe. Mrs. E. [illegible]rkin, 137 Alfred-Rd. Sheffield.	do. do.

24th. M. The day passed quietly. The Doctor came round twice. Meals very good.

25th. Tu. Went to the operating room on a Ruskis back to be dressed. The Doctor said I would have to rest in bed. The Sgt. brot a sandbag for me to rest on my ????[base?] so as to straighten the leg.

26th. W. The Sgt. fm the Lager Camp came round in the afternoon & picturised[??] us a parcel on the moisers[???].

27th. Th. Received a pcl each containing 3 tins of Bully & 2 tins of roast, 1or2 small tins of cheese, 1 tin of Dripping, 4 pckts of biscuits, ¼ lb of cocoa & 2 sm tins of Nestles from the boys at Lager Camp.

28th. Fr. G. Sgt. came round for pay books. I did not give him mine. Gave him a 2 phennig piece for exchange into G[erman] money. Particulars[my extension of an abbreviation] taken on a card including home address. Wrote 2 p.c.s (home & to Red Cross) ackng. pcl. Asked mother to send 2/6 to Wills each Wed.

29th. Sa. Sgt. collected p.c. but wld only take one besides the one to Red Cross. Went into the pound on crutches.

30th. Su. Good dinner of fried potatoes & froad[fried?] beef, gravy & macaroni soup. Went out again into the grounds[?] on crutches. Found a nest of mice & the mother mouse in the mattress of Ginger's bed.

The Notebook

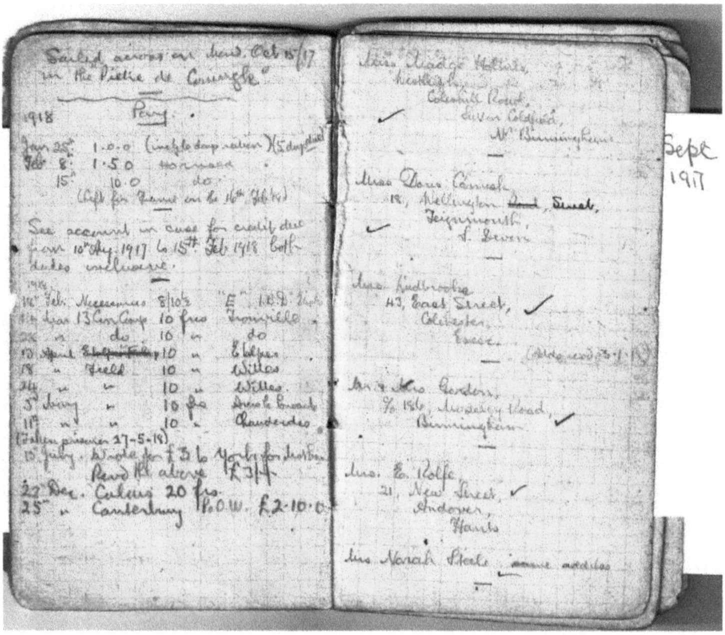

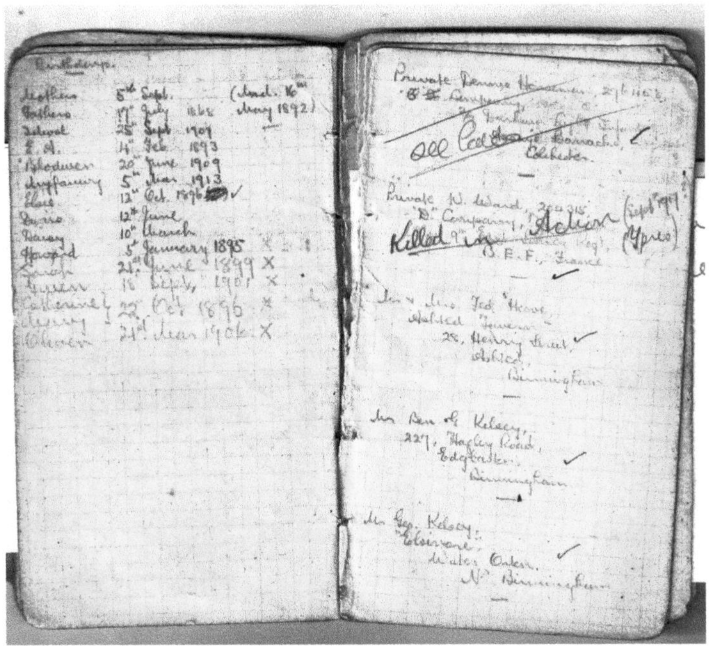

Birthdays.

Mothers 5th Sept. (Married 16th May 1892)
Fathers 17th July 1868
School 25th Sept 1907
E. A. 4th Feb 1893
Rhodesia 20th June 1909
12th Oct. 1896 ✓
12th June
10th March
5th January 1895
21st June 1899 X
16 Sept, 1901 X
Catherine 22 Oct 1896
21st Mar 1906 X

Private W. Ward, 200315
"D" Company,
Killed in Action (Sept 1917 Ypres)
B.E.F., France ✓

Mr & Mrs Ted Howe,
28, Henry Street, ✓
Birmingham

Mr Ben G Kelsey,
227, Hagley Road,
Edgbaston, ✓
Birmingham

Mr Geo. Kelsey,
Water Orton. ✓
Nr Birmingham

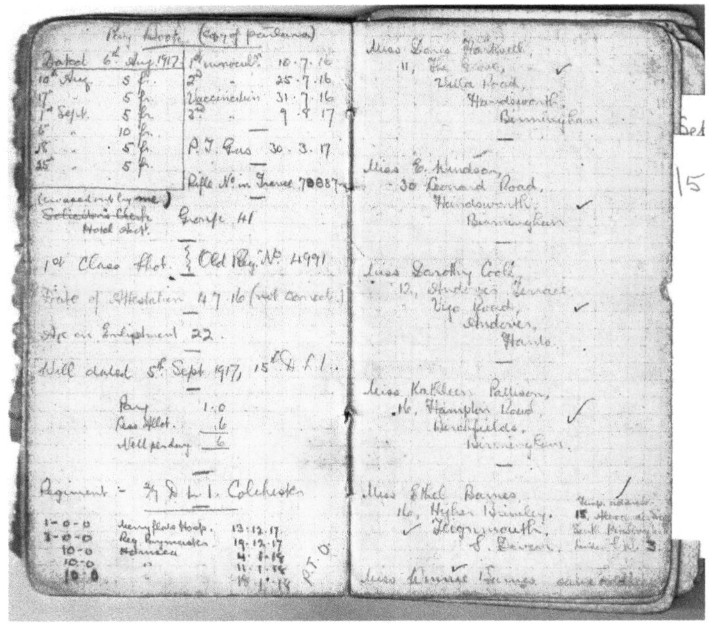

Pay Book (copy of particulars)

Dated 6th Aug 1917	
10th Aug.	5 fr.
17th "	5 fr.
1st Sept.	5 fr.
6th "	10 fr.
18 "	5 fr.
25 "	5 fr.

1st inoculation 10.7.16
2nd " 25.7.16
Vaccination 31.7.16
2nd " 9.8.17

P. T. Gas 30.3.17

Rifle No in France 70887

Hotel Clerk. Group 41

1st Class Shot. Old Reg. No 4991

Date of Attestation 4.7.16 (not correct.)

Age on Enlistment 22.

Will dated 5th Sept 1917, 15th D L I..

Pay 1.0
Less Allot. .6
6

Regiment :- 2/7 D. L. I. Colchester

1-0-0		13.12.17
3-0-0	Reg. Paymaster	19.12.17
10-0		4.1.18
10-0		11.1.18
10-0		18.1.18

P.T.O.

Miss Doris Hartwell,
11, The Grove, ✓
Villa Road,
Handsworth,
Birmingham

Miss E. Knudsen,
30 Leonard Road,
Handsworth, ✓
Birmingham

Miss Dorothy Cook,
12, Andover Terrace
Vigo Road, ✓
Andover,
Hants.

Miss Kathleen Pattison,
16, Hampton Road ✓
Birchfields,
Birmingham.

Miss Ethel Barnes,
16, Higher Brimley.
✓ Teignmouth.
S. Devon.

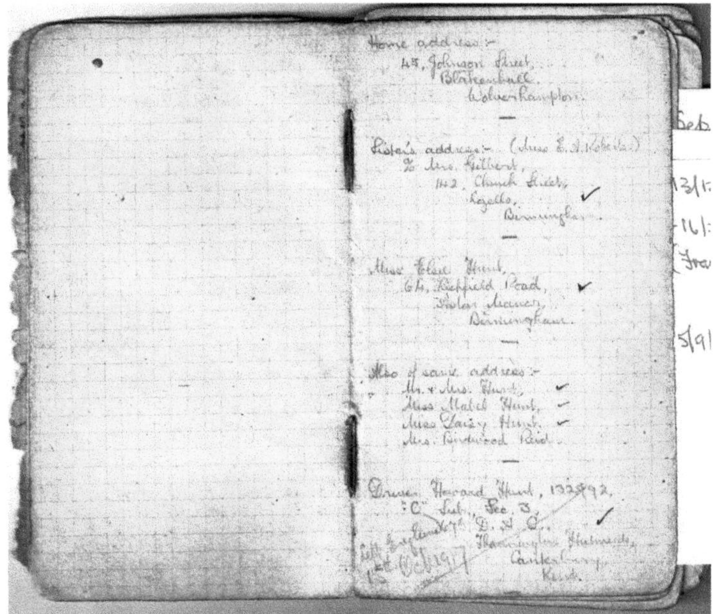

Home address:–
45, Johnson Street,
Blakenhall,
Wolverhampton.

Sister's address:– (Miss E. A. Roberts)
% Mrs. Gilbert,
142, Church Street,
Lozells,
Birmingham.

Miss Elsie Hunt,
64, Lichfield Road,
Aston Manor,
Birmingham.

Also of same address:–
Mr. & Mrs. Hunt,
Miss Mabel Hunt,
Miss Daisy Hunt.
Mrs. Birdwood Reid.

Driver Howard Hunt, 132892,
"C" Sub., Sec. 3,
7th D. A. C.
Canterbury,
Kent.

Left England 1st Oct 1917

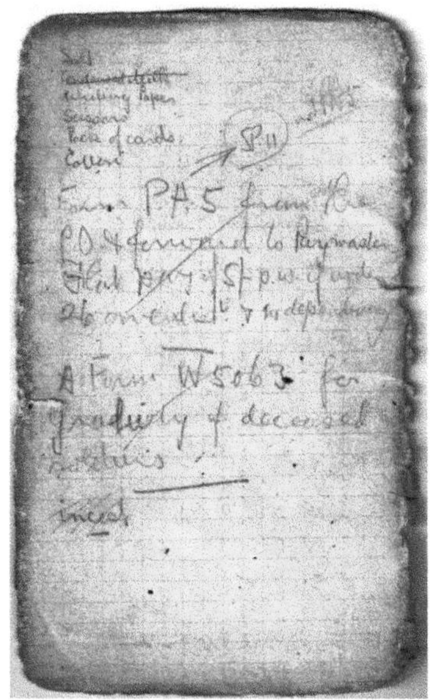

Writing Paper
Scissors
Pack of cards.
Cover

P.11

Form P.A.5 from the P.O. & forward to Paymaster

A Form W 5063 for gratuity of deceased soldiers

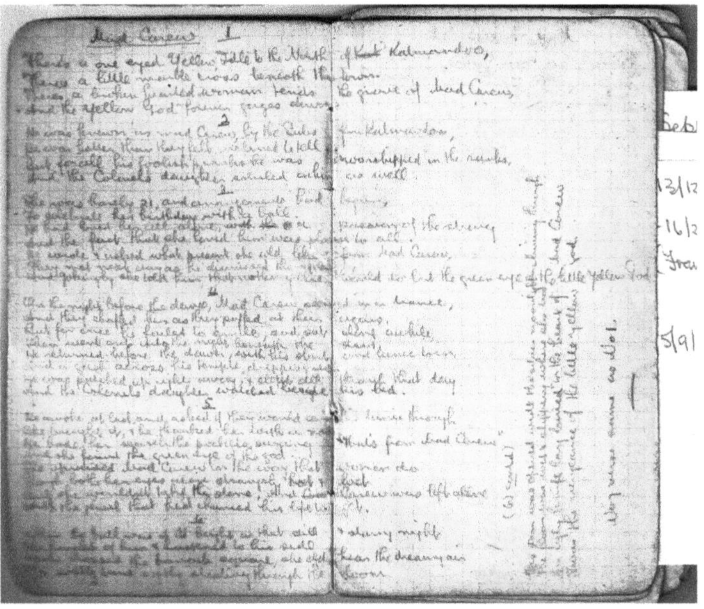

Private W.J.G. Roberts,
278410 "B" Company,
15th Durham L.I. Inf'y,
B.E.F., France, 19.9.17.

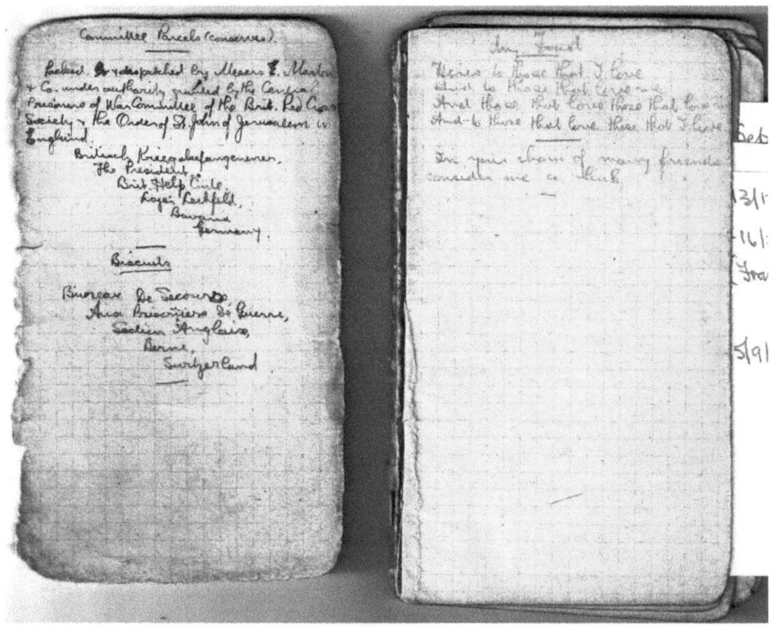

Committee Parcels (conserves).

Packed & despatched by Messrs F. Mason & Co. under authority granted by the Central Prisoners of War Committee of the Brit. Red Cross Society & the Order of St. John of Jerusalem in England.

Britisch Kriegsgefangenen,
The President,
Brit. Help Circle,
Lager Lechfeld,
Bavaria
Germany.

Biscuits

Bureau de Secours
Aux Prisonniers de Guerre,
Section Anglaise,
Berne,
Switzerland

My Toast

Here's to those that I love
And to those that love me
And those that love those that love me
And to those that love those that I love

In your chain of many friends
consider me a link.

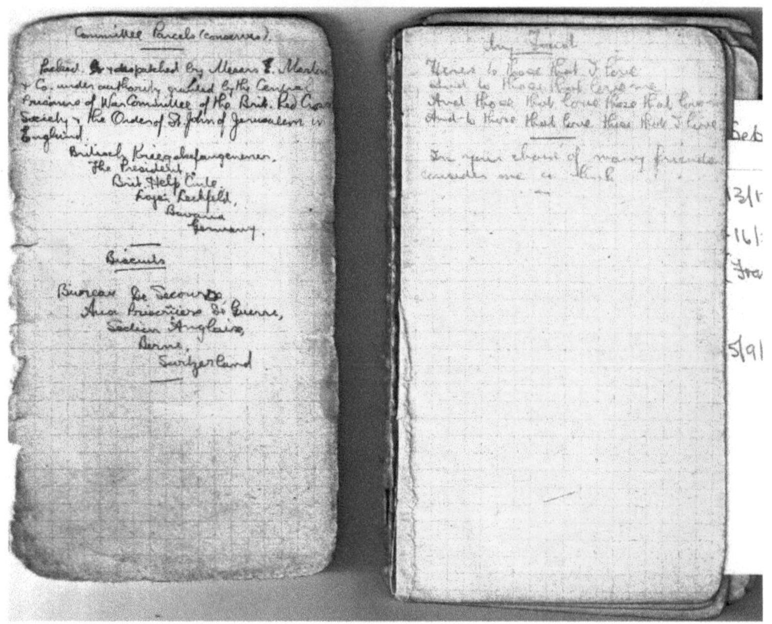

Committee Parcels (conserves).

Packed & despatched by Messrs F. Mason & Co. under authority granted by the Central Prisoners of War Committee of the Brit. Red Cross Society & the Order of St. John of Jerusalem in England.

Britisch Kriegsgefangenen,
The President,
Brit. Help Circle,
Lager Lechfeld,
Bavaria
Germany.

Biscuits

Bureau de Secours
Aux Prisonniers de Guerre,
Section Anglaise,
Berne,
Switzerland

My Toast

Here's to those that I love
And to those that love me
And those that love those that love me
And to those that love those that I love

In your chain of many friends
consider me a link.

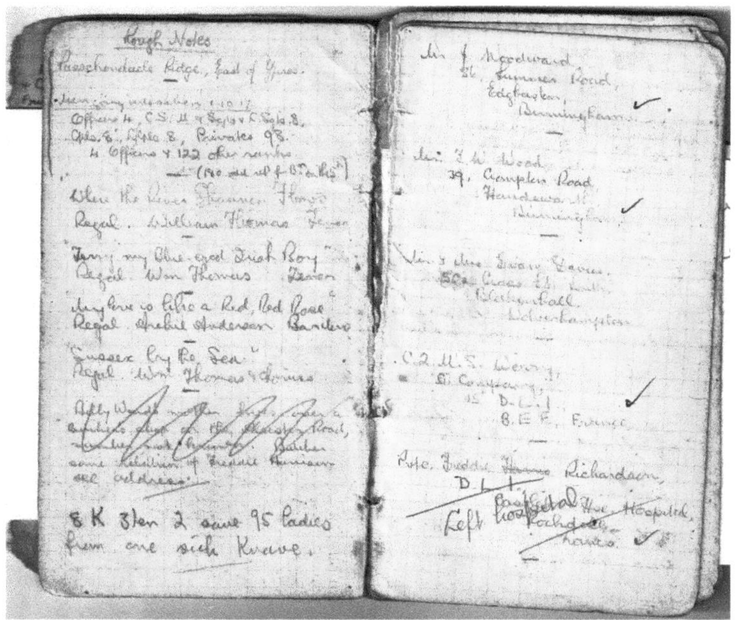

Rough Notes

Passchendaele Ridge, East of Ypres.

Officers 4, C.S.M. 4 Sgts & L Sgts 8,
Cpls. 8, L/Cpls 8, Privates 98.
4 Officers & 122 other ranks

"When the River Shannon Flows"
Regal. William Thomas Tenor

"Terry my Blue-eyed Irish Boy"
Regal. Wm Thomas Tenor

"My love is like a Red, Red Rose"
Regal. Archie Anderson Baritone

"Sussex by the Sea"
Regal. Wm Thomas & Chorus

8 K 3ten 2 save 95 ladies
from one such Knave.

Mr J. Woodward
26, Sumner Road,
Edgbaston,
Birmingham.

Mr E. W. Wood
39, Crompton Road
Handsworth
Birmingham.

C.Q.M.S. Berry
D Company
15 D.L.I.
B.E.F. France

Pte. Freddie Richardson,
D.L.I.
Left hospital

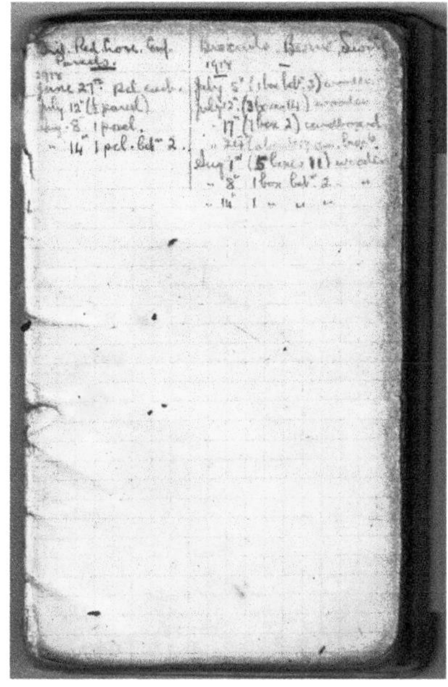

Red Cross. Parcels.	
1918	1918
June 27th Red card.	July 5th (1 box lot 3)
July 12th (1 parcel)	July 12th (3 ...)
Aug. 8 1 parcel.	" 17th (1 box 2) cardboard
" 14th 1 pcl. lot 2.	Aug 1st (5 boxes 11)
	" 8th 1 box lot 2 "
	" 14th 1 " " "

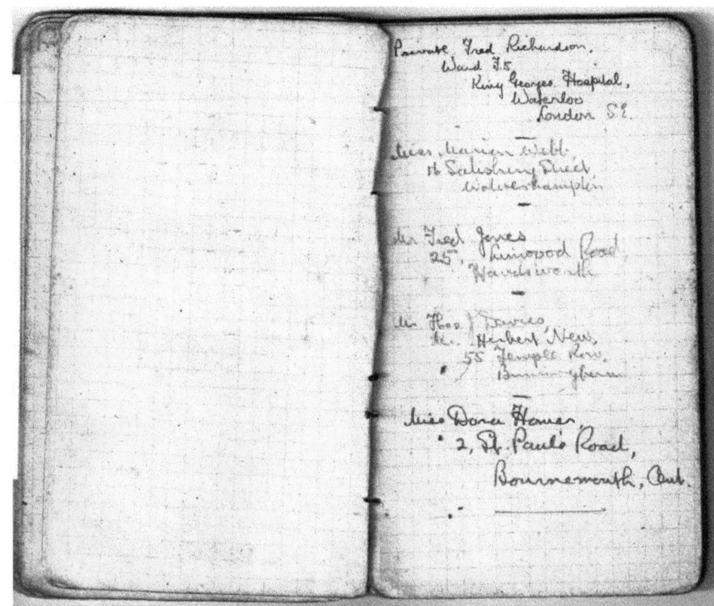

Private Fred Richardson,
Ward F.5
King Georges Hospital,
Waterloo
London S.E.

Miss Marian Webb,
16 Salisbury Street
Wolverhampton

Mr Fred Jones
25, Linwood Road,
Wandsworth

Mr Thos J Davies,
Herbert New,
55 Temple Row,
Birmingham

Miss Dora Homer,
2, St. Paul's Road,
Bournemouth

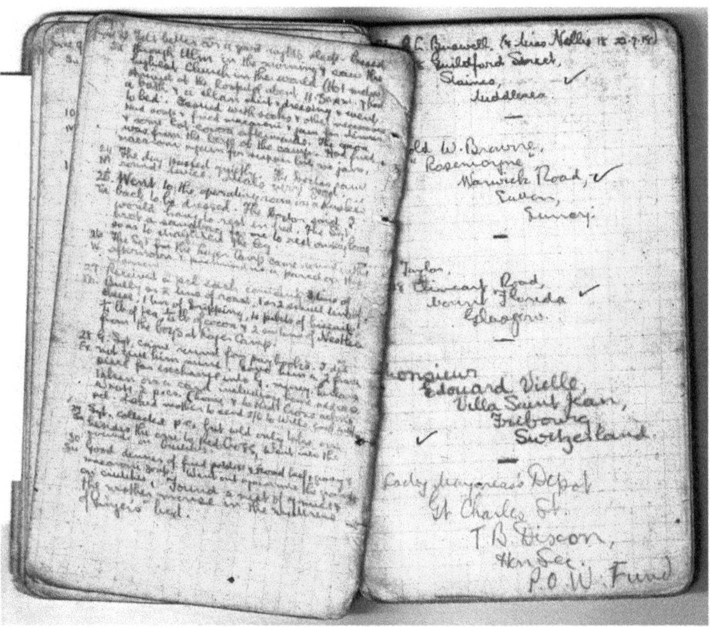

Guildford Street,
Staines,
Middlesex

W. Browne,
Warwick Road,
Surrey

Taylor,
Glasgow

Monsieur
Edouard Vielle,
Villa Saint Jean,
Fribourg
Switzerland

Lady Mayoress's Depot
St Charles St.
T.B. Dixon,
Hon Sec.
P.O.W. Fund

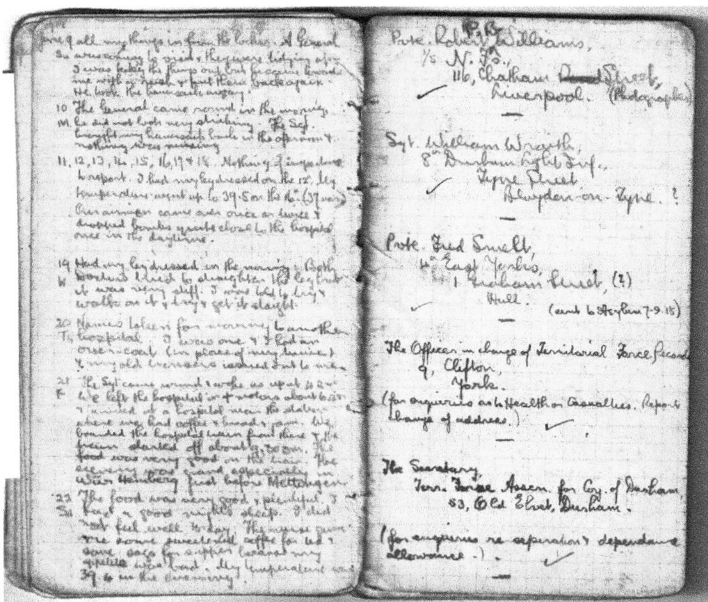

June 9 all my things in from the locker. A General
Su was coming to visit & they were tidying up.
I was taking the things out but he came towards
me with a [illegible] & put them back again.
He took the haversack away.

10 The General came round in the morning.
M. He did not look very striking. The Sgt.
brought my haversack back in the afternoon &
nothing was missing.

11, 12, 13, 14, 15, 16, 17 & 18. Nothing of importance
to report. I had my leg dressed on the 12th. My
temperature went up to 39.5 on the 16th (37 norm)
Our airmen came over once or twice &
dropped bombs quite close to the hospital
once in the daytime.

19 Had my leg dressed in the morning. Both
W doctors tried to straighten the leg but
it was very stiff. I was told to try &
walk on it & try & get it straight.

20 Names taken for moving to another
Th hospital. I was one & I had an
over-coat (in place of my tunic)
& my old trousers issued out to me.

21 The Sgt came round & woke us up at 4 a.m.
F We left the hospital in motors about 6 a.m.
& waited at a hospital near the station
where we had coffee & bread & jam. We
boarded the hospital train from there & the
train started off about 7.30 a.m. The
food was very good on the train. The
scenery was grand especially in
[illegible] Hamburg just before Mettingen.

22 The food was very good & plentiful. I
Sa had a good night's sleep. I did
not feel well today. The nurse gave
me some sweetened coffee for tea &
some [illegible] for supper because my
appetite was bad. My temperature was
39.6 in the evening.

Pte. Robert Williams,
1/5 N. Fs.,
116, Chatham ~~Road~~ Street,
Liverpool. (Photographer)

Sgt. William Wrath,
8th Durham Light Inf.,
Tyne Street
Blaydon-on-Tyne. ?

Pte. Fred Smelt,
4th East Yorks,
1 Graham Street, (?)
Hull. (sent to Asylum 7-9-15)

The Officer in charge of Territorial Force Records
9, Clifton,
York.
(for enquiries as to Health or Casualties. Report change of address.)

The Secretary,
Terr. Force Assn. for Cy. of Durham
53, Old Elvet, Durham.

(for enquiries re separation & dependance allowance.)

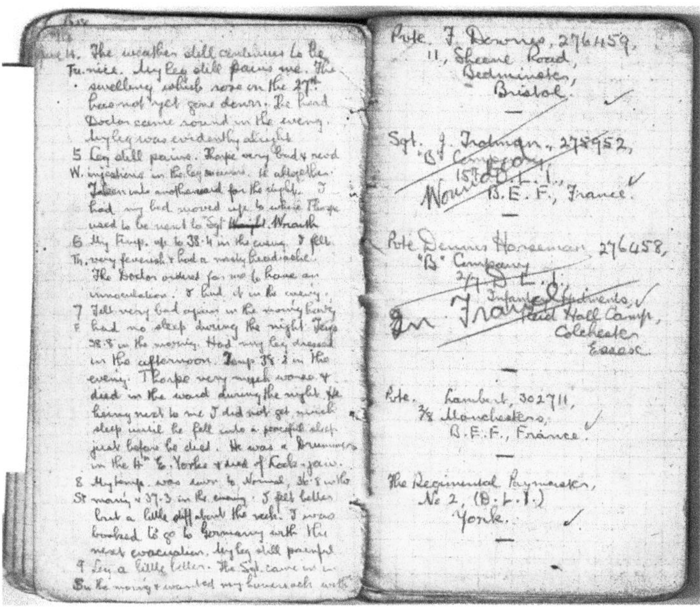

June 4. The weather still continues to be
Tu. nice. My leg still pains me. The
swelling which rose on the 27th
has not yet gone down. The head
Doctor came round in the evening.
My leg was evidently alright

5 Leg still pains. Thorpe very bad & needs
W. injections in the leg [illegible]. He altogether
taken into another ward for the night. I
had my bed moved up to where Thorpe
used to be next to Sgt ~~Knight~~ Wrath

6 My temp. up to 38.4 in the evening. I felt
Th. very feverish & had a nasty headache.
The Doctor ordered for me to have an
innoculation. I had it in the evening.

7 Felt very bad again in the morning having
F had no sleep during the night. Temp
38.8 in the morning. Had my leg dressed
in the afternoon. Temp 38.2 in the
evening. Thorpe very much worse &
died in the ward during the night. He
being next to me I did not get much
sleep until he fell into a peaceful sleep
just before he died. He was a Drummer
in the 4th E. Yorks & died of lock-jaw.

8 My temp. was down to Normal, 36.8 in the
St morning & 37.3 in the evening. I felt better
but a little stiff about the neck. I was
booked to go to Germany with the
next evacuation. My leg still painful

9 Leg a little better. The Sgt. came in in
Su the morning & wanted my haversack with

Pte. J. Downs, 276459.
11, Sheene Road,
Bedminster,
Bristol.

Sgt. J. Trainor, 275952,
~~"B" Company~~
~~15th D.L.I.~~
~~B.E.F., France.~~
Wounded

Pte Dennis Horseman 276458,
"B" Company
~~2/7 D.L.I.~~
~~Infantry Reinforcements,~~
~~Reed Hall Camp,~~
~~Colchester~~
~~Essex.~~
In France

Pte. Lambert, 302711,
3/8 Manchesters,
B.E.F., France.

The Regimental Paymaster,
No 2, (D.L.I.)
York.

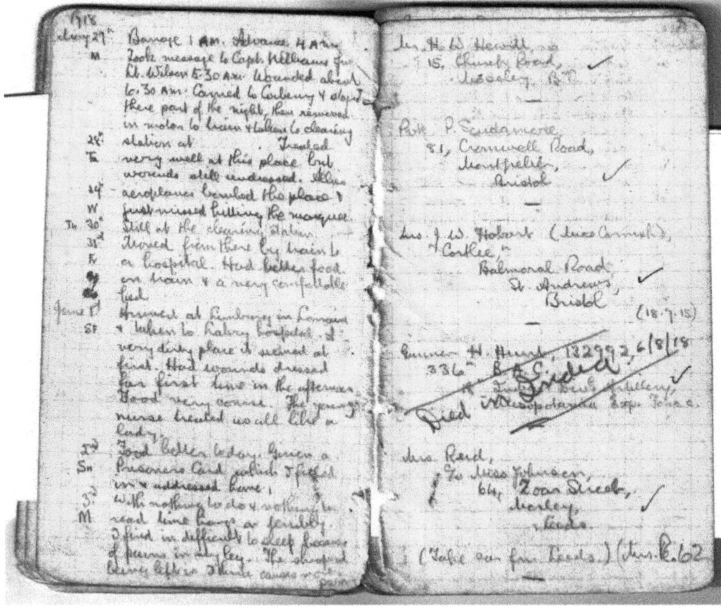

1918
May 27th M Barrage 1 AM. Advance 4 AM.
Took message to Capt. Williams for
Lt. Wilson 5.30 AM. Wounded about
6.30 AM. Carried to Corbeny & stayed
there part of the night, then removed
in motor to train & taken to clearing
28th Tu station at . Treated
very well at this place but
wounds still undressed. Allies
29th W aeroplanes bombed the place &
just missed hitting the marquee.
Th 30th Still at the clearing station.
31st Fr Moved from there by train to
a hospital. Had better food
on train & a very comfortable
bed.
June 1st St Arrived at [illegible] in [illegible]
& taken to [illegible] hospital. A
very dirty place it seemed at
first. Had wounds dressed
for first time in the afternoon.
Food very coarse. The young
nurse treated us all like a
lady.
2nd Sn Food better today. Given a
Prisoners Card which I filled
in & addressed home.
3rd M With nothing to do & nothing to
read time hangs so terribly.
I find it difficult to sleep because
of pains in my leg. The [illegible]
[illegible] I think causes [illegible] pain

Mrs. H. W. Hewitt,
15, [illegible] Road,
[illegible], B'm ✓

Pte. P. Scudamore,
81, Cromwell Road,
Montpelier,
Bristol ✓

Mrs. J. W. Hobart (Miss Cornish),
"Corlee,"
Balmoral Road,
St. Andrews,
Bristol ✓
(18.7.15)

~~Gunner H. Hunt, 132992, 6/8/18~~
~~336th B. A. C.~~
~~R. F. [illegible] Artillery,~~ ✓
~~Mesopotamia Exp. Force.~~
Died

Mrs. Reid,
c/o Miss Johnson,
64, Zoar Street,
Morley,
Leeds. ✓

("Take car for Leeds.) (Mrs. R. 62

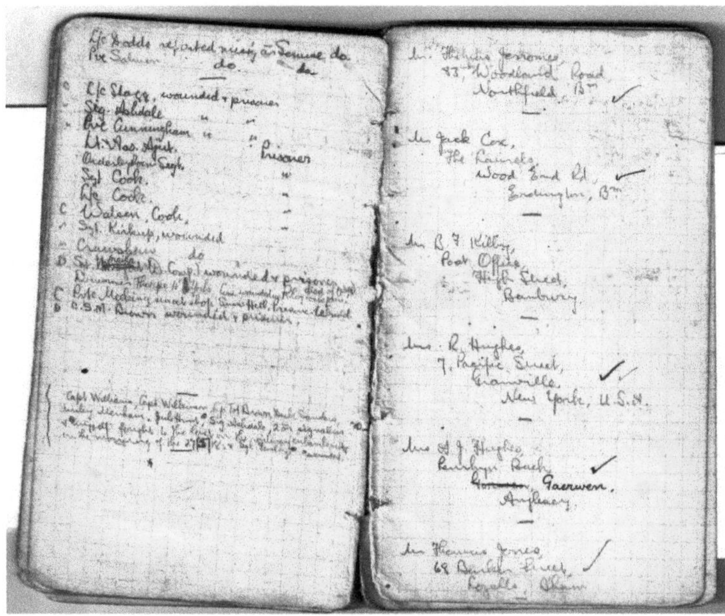

L/c Dodds reported missing in Somme do
Pte Salmon do. do

C L/c Stagg, wounded & prisoner
Sig. Abdale " "
Pte Cunningham " " Prisoner
Lt. & Qas. Agut.
Orderly Room Sergt.
Sgt Cook. "
L/c Cooke. "
C Watson, Cook, "
Sgt. Kirkup, wounded "
Crawshaw do
D Sgt ~~[illegible]~~ (D. Coy.) wounded & prisoner
Drummer Thorpe [illegible] [illegible] died of [illegible]
C Pte Medking [illegible] [illegible] Prisoner [illegible]
D C.S.M. Brown wounded & prisoner,

Capt. Williams, Capt. Wilkinson [illegible] [illegible] [illegible]
[illegible] [illegible] [illegible] Sig. Abdale, 2 [illegible] signallers
& myself fought to the last [illegible] [illegible]
in the morning of the 27/5/18. & Sgt [illegible] wounded.

Mr. [illegible] Jeromes,
83, Woodland Road
Northfield, B'm ✓

Mr. Jack Cox,
The Laurels,
Wood End Rd,
Erdington, B'm ✓

Mr. B. F. Kilby,
Post Office,
High Street,
Banbury

Mrs. R. Hughes,
7, Pacific Street,
Granville
New York, U.S.A. ✓

Mrs. A. J. Hughes,
[illegible] [illegible],
~~[illegible]~~, Gaerwen.
Anglesey ✓

Mr. Thomas Jones,
68 [illegible] Street,
[illegible], Oldham ✓

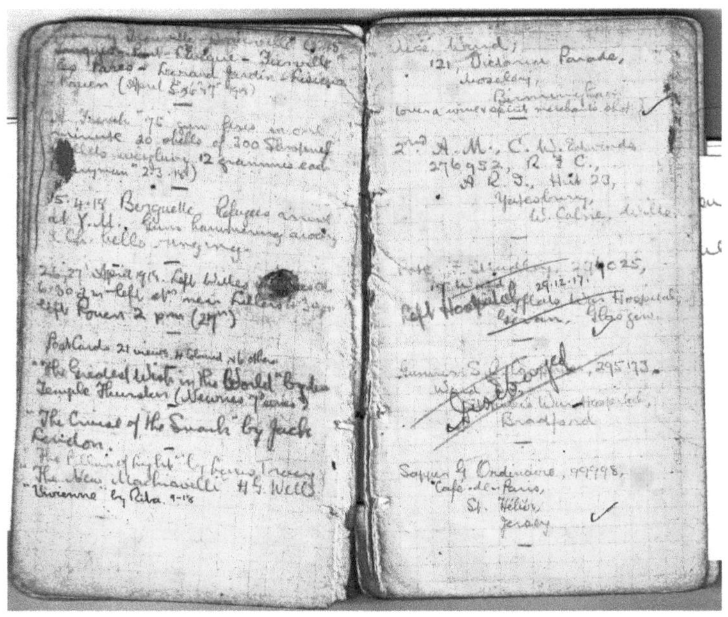

A French "75" gun fires in one minute 20 shells of 300 Shrapnel bullets weighing 12 grammes each [illegible] 23.3.18)

15.4.18 Bezquelle. Refugees arrive at Y.M. Guns hammering away & Ch. bells ringing.

[illegible]

Left Rouen 2 p.m. (27th)

"The Greatest Wish in the World" by E. Temple Thurston (Newnes [illegible])

"The Cruise of the Snark" by Jack London.

"The New Machiavelli" H.G. Wells

"Vivienne" by Rita. 9-18

121, Victoria Parade, Moseley, Birmingham.

2nd A.M., C.W. Edwards 276952, R.F.C., [illegible] Hut 23, Yatesbury, W. Calne, Wilts.

Sapper G. [illegible], 99998, Café de Paris, St. Helier, Jersey

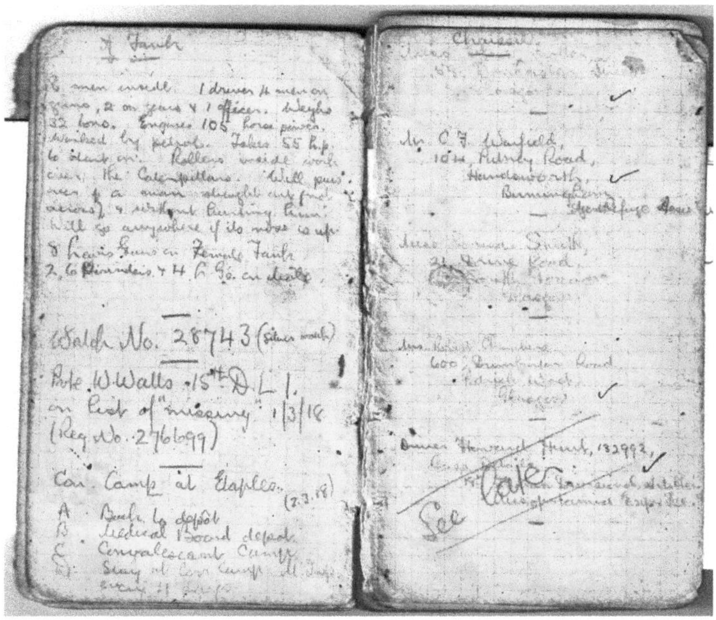

Tank

8 men inside. 1 driver 4 men on guns, 2 on gears & 1 officer. Weighs 32 tons. Engines 105 horse power. Worked by petrol. Takes 55 h.p. to start it. [illegible] Will go anywhere if its nose is up. 8 Lewis Guns in Female Tank 2, 6 Pounders & 4 L. Gs. in Male

Watch No. 28743 (silver watch)

Pte. W. Watts 15th D.L.I. on list of "missing" 1/3/18 (Reg. No. 276699)

Con. Camp at Etaples (2.3.18)

A. Back to depot
B. Medical Board depot
C. Convalescent Camp
[illegible]

Mr. C.F. Warfield, [illegible] Road, Handsworth, Birmingham

[illegible]

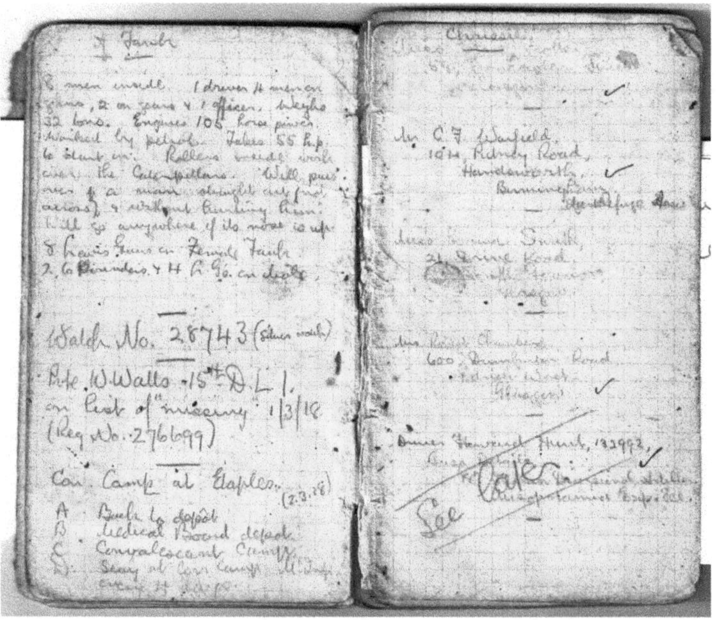

Of Tanks

8 men inside. 1 driver 4 men on guns, 2 on gears & 1 officer. Weighs 32 tons. Engines 105 horse power worked by petrol. Takes 55 h.p. to start up. Rollers inside work over the Caterpillars. Will pass over [illegible] of a man straight out (not across) & without hurting him. Will go anywhere if its nose is up.
8 Lewis Guns on Female Tank
2. 6 Pounders & 4 L. Gs. on Male

Watch No. 28743 (silver watch)

Pte. W. Watts 15th D.L.I.
on list of "missing" 1/3/18
(Reg No. 276699)

Con. Camp at Etaples. (2.3.18)
A. Back to depot
B. Medical Board depot
C. Convalescent Camp
D. Stay at Con Camp [illegible]

[illegible]

Mr. C. F. Warfield,
104, [illegible] Road,
Handsworth,
Birmingham.

Miss [illegible] Smith,
21 [illegible] Road,
[illegible]

Mrs [illegible] Chambers
600, [illegible] Road
[illegible]
Glasgow

[illegible]
See later

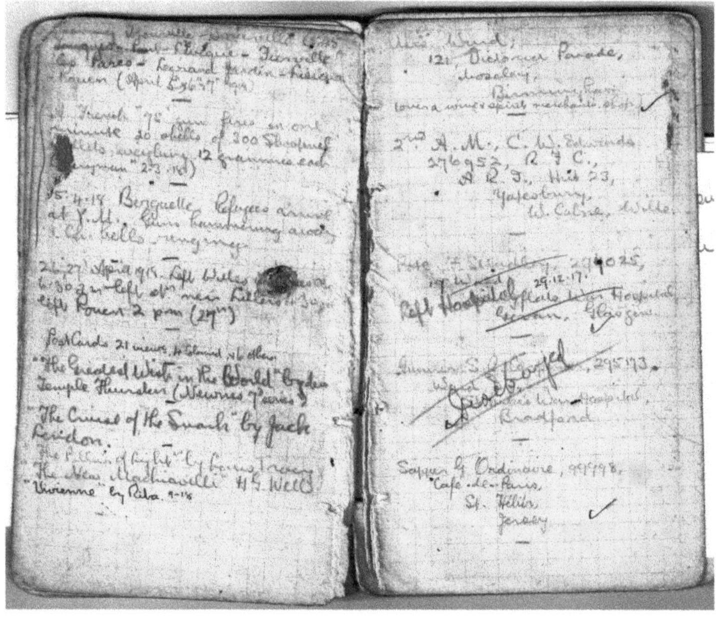

[illegible] Paris – [illegible] Rouen (April [illegible])

A French "75" gun fires in one minute 20 shells of 300 Shrapnel bullets, weighing 12 grammes each [illegible] (2-3-18)

15.4.18 Bezquelle. Refugees arrive at Y.M. Guns hammering away & ch. bells ringing.

26/27 April 9.18. Left [illegible] 6.30 p.m. left [illegible] Left Rouen 2 pm (27th)

PostCards 21 views, 4 Island, 16 other

"The Greatest Wish in the World" by E. Temple Thurston (Newnes Paris)
"The Curse of the Snake" by Jack Leedon.
"The Pillar of Light" by Louis Tracy
"The New Machiavelli" H.G. Wells
"Vivienne" by Rita. 9-18

Miss Ward,
121, Victoria Parade,
Moseley,
Birmingham

2nd A.M., C. W. Edwards
276952, R F C.,
A. R. S., Hut 23,
Yatesbury,
W. Calne, Wilts.

[illegible]
Left Hospital

[illegible]
Bradford

Sapper G. Ordinaire, 99998,
"Café de Paris,
St. Helier,
Jersey

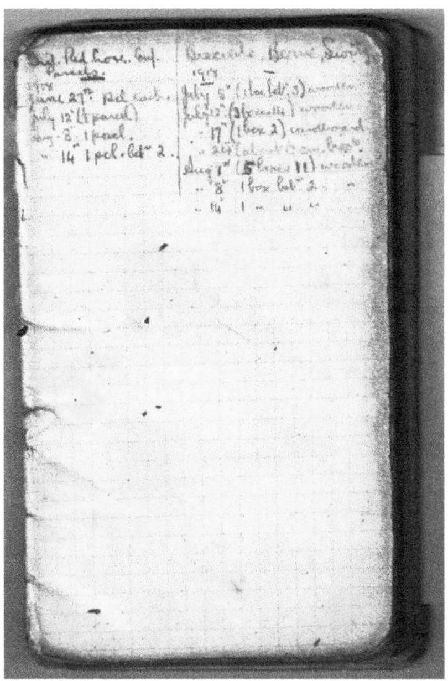

Also within this note book working from the upturned rear are the following summaries:–

1918

Feb. 16. Left Hornsea 5.15 pm.

17 Arrd. Folkestone 6am.

Arrd. Boulonge (St. Martin's Camp)

18 Left Boulonge 8am.

Arrd. Etaples (Eth J.B.D.)

19. Admitted to Marquee (sick).

20. Admitted to Ward 27A, 5 bed, 24th General Hospital.

Mar. 2. Left 24th General Hospital. Admitted to 6th Convalescent Depot at Etaples.

3. Left No.6 Con. Camp.

4. Arrived at Trouville & went on to No. 13 Convalescent Depot, Deauville.

Apr. 5. Left Trouville. Stopped at Lisieux.

6. Arrd. Ar Rouen 7.30am. Left Rouen 2.30pm.

7. Arrd. At Etaples. Taken to M.B. Depot.

10. Marked A at Medical Board. Met Stafford at 'E' Depot.

13. Dennis Horseman arrived at Base.

[A photograph of D. Horseman with P. Scudamore and A.Shell is included below. I'm guessing that he is on the left.]

Apr. 14. Saw him in the morning.

Apr. 14. Left Etaples about 5.30pm for the line.

15. Arrived at Berguelle about 3am. Left for AIR about 11.30am. Went thro' AIR & arrived at Reinforcement Camp at Mathes 1.15pm.

17 Left Mathes [Nathes?] 11am & arrived at Willes 2.30pm.

26. Left Willes in Motor buses about 5.30am.[39] Entrained at a station beyond Lillers about 4pm.

27. Passed through Rouen. Went round Paris

28. Arrived at a siding & marched to Arcis-le-Ponsart[40] to our billets.

May 5. Left Arcis-le-Ponsart 5.30am. Passed through Fismes. Arrived at destinations a distance of about 18 kilos, nr Brislieux.[41]

7. Left for Reserves about 12.10am.

13. Left Chauderdes [Chaudardes?] (reserves) about 10.30pm.

14. Arrived in Supports, Trenches Saussien.

19. Went into front line on Craonne Plateau.

25. Went back into Supports (Trenches Saussien).

27. Wounded & taken prisoner.

28. Taken to clearing station.

31. Removed from clearing station.

June 1. Arrived in hospital at Limburg(Labry) Lorraine. Had wounds dressed for first time.

June 21.Left Limburg Hosp. Lorrain.[no 'e']

23. Arrived at Lajer[42] Lechfeld Hospital.

39 Did he use a capital M for Motor because at that time they were still relatively new?

40 Due south of Fismes.

41 Does he mean Baslieux?

42 Later it is spelt Lager.

Sept 13. Left Lazarell & arrv'd at Lajer.

27. Had tooth out at Rivier.

30. Fumagation [his spelling] & bath.

Oct 17. Recd. 1st Biscuit pcl fm Berne.

Oct 22. Recd. 1st Regl. Conserve Pcl.

Nov 8. Bavarian soldiers take over charge of the camp from the military authorities. No fighting took place.

16. Recd. the first news of Howard's death from Elsie. The first letter she wrote arrived on Nov 19th.

1918

Nov 29. Went to the Camp Cinema with Jock & Tiny.

30. Went to Kloster Lechfeld with the Sgt. Major's party. Had drinks. Bou't pick post cards. Had a look inside the Kloster. Went to a Russian Service in the evening with Harold & Aydon.

Dec 3. Went to Kloster Lechfeld with Harold. Went over the Shrine.

5 Went to Lechfeld & then to Kloster Lechfeld with Jock & Matheson. Went inside the Kloster.

7. Went to the funeral of an Australian & Englishman(Lewis & Barnal). Saw the memorial of 1870-1 to the French Soldiers who died while Prisoners of War at Lechfeld. Went on to Kloster Lechfeld with Jock afterwards. Went to the pictures at 9 o'clock with Harold & Tiny.

Below are two photographs of a ceremony inside a camp which could be of the funeral referred to.

I now return to the running diaries continuing from the comment on the mice in Ginger's bed on 30th June 1918.

July 1st. M. Went out on crutches to another barrack to ???[use?] Senior. Raining most of the day. Saw a German's military funeral[this most certainly clarifies the subject matter of the photographs referred to previously].

Tu.2nd. Raining nearly all day. Gave George a tin of milk for a 4/- postal order dated 9th May 1918.

W. 3rd.Heavy rain all day. Gave George one of the 5 p.cs. Had frog & snail soup for supper.

Th. 4th. Raining heavily all day. Gave the young orderly a tin of cocoa(1/4lb) for a metal cigarette case. The Sgt. came round f'm Lager Camp& brought us a YMCA pamphlet.Sd biscuit parcels would come round on the morrow. Told me it was impossible to get a postal order changed.

Fr. 5th. Lovely weather. Went out into the grounds after dinner & stayed up until about 8.30. Biscuits arrived about 3.30, I box between 3, some had 11 biscuits & some 17 & 20. Called at No. 22 barrack. Had my weight taken. 49Kgs (about 110 1/4 lbs).

Sat. 6th. George bat. me 2 cigs for 30ph. I had a warm argument with the young Jerry orderly about dishing out the coffee for bfst. I threatened I wld tell the Dr. Young Black gave me a cigarette; he got 30 for his cocoa. I got up a bit in the afternoon & I had a bit of a feint & had to be carried back to bed.

Sun. 7th. Lovely weather. Had a good dinner of soup, meat & fried potatoes & gravy & blanc mange. Got up after dinner & went out into the grounds. Had a good supper of vegetable soup. Had a shave in the evening.

Mon. 8th. The Dr. came round in the morning & told all the Englishmen (except me) that they could go out into the sunshine. He messed about trying to straighten my leg. I got up & went outside. Had a good dinner of soup & meat & fried potatoes & gravy. The Sgt called round from Lager Camp. Gave us a cigarette each. (Potatoe soup for supper).

Tues. 9th. Got up in the morning. Lovely weather. Meatless day. Heavy thunderstorm at night. (Semolina for supper).

Wed. 10th. Got up in the morning & had a game of dominoes. Good dinner, stewed potatoes & meat. (Macaroni& stewed fruit for supper).

Thurs. 11th. Parcels arrive at the office but are not dished out. Had a game of dominoes in the afternoon. Craut [sauerkraut?] for supper.

Fri. 12th. Did not get up until after dinner. Macaroni & jam & a good soup for dinner. Semolina for supper. Parcels issued out at 6pm. One parcel of conserves between 2 & three boxes of biscuits between 14. Re'vd 8 biscuits each. All tinned stuff kept at the office to be opened there to search for any information that may be sent through. All labels are even taken off the tinned milk & c. Smoked some dry leaves because I couldn't get tobacco or cigs. The doctor examined & made reports of everybody's wounds.

1918

July 13th.

Sat. English speaking Jerry came round from Lager for some information as to addresses & e[?] from some of the lads & gave Warrington & myself German cash for our Eng. & French money.I received 1mark 50ph. For a 2 franc piece. Warrington received 2 mark 65phen. For 2/6. He sd all Eng. money had to go to Berlin for exchange. French money cld be exchanged at a French p.o. in the camp. Our hut (Bnk 3) scrubbed out in the afternoon. Meat & spinach & potatoes for dinner, vegetable soup for supper. Wrote p.c. to Yorks Paydr[Paymaster?] for Sinden.

I include next examples of the 'money' used in the POW camp and an image of what appears to be the nearest town, Augsburg, which at the time had a population of just over 100,000.

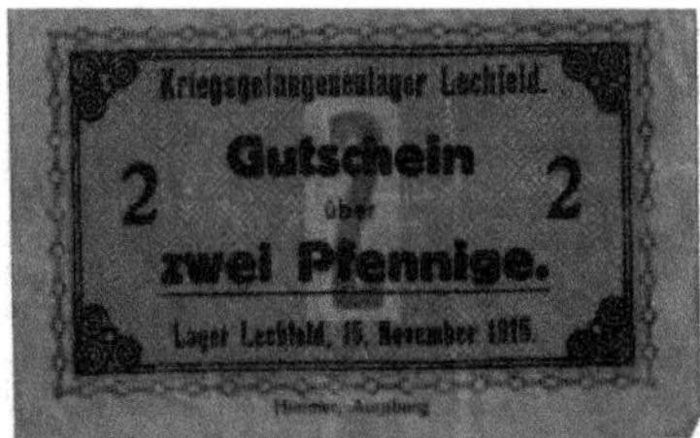

Sun. 14th. Got up in the morning. Bought 8 cigs for 1 mark. Geo. Sinton & I smoked them between us. Sat talking in bed until nearly 1am at night. Charlie, the Jerry from the cook house came in & talked to us tioice[??twice??]. Gave George a cob of bread. Dried some leaves for smoking. George begged me a pipe of baccee.

Mon. 15th. Had one cig left; had a draw of it before bfst & Geo. Finished afr bfst while I smoked the baccee he gave me. Poor dinner of tongue & sour crout. Stewed fruit & macaroni for supper.

Tues.16th. Got up in the morning just afr bfst. Our boys did the work in the ward & took round instead of the Ruskies. Soup, macaroni and jam for dinner. Pololina for supper.

Wed. 17th. Drew the last of the tinned stuff from the office. Biscuits arriving, 1 box between two. I had 27. Meat & mashed cabbage & sliced cabbage storks for dinner. Stinking cheese & roast spuds for supper. Weighed in the morning at 52K.(47 last time).

Thurs. 18th. Revd. 30 cigs for tea. In shares with Black. Gave 3 biscuits for some good dried leaves for smoking. Had a game of Solo in the evening. Macaroni, soup & meat & gravy for dinner. Potatoe soup for supper. Gave a biscuit for a cigarette holder from a Ruskie.

Fri. 19th. Played solo in the morning. Spinach & fried potatoes, meat & soup for dinner. Roast potatoes & stinking cheese for supper.

Sat. 20th. Soup & sour crout & meat for dinner, consertince for supper. Played solo in the evening.

Sun. 21st. Soup, meat & c for dinner, read "The Greater Power" by Harold Bindloss afr dinner. Roast potatoes & cheese for supper. Exchanged biscuit for cigarette.

Mond. 22nd. Read "The Greatest Wish in the World" by Mrs. Temple Thurston [E Temple Thurston]. Soup, meat & gravy, potatoes for dinner. Roast spuds & cheese for supper. Sold 4 biscuits for 1 mark.

Tues. 23rd. Pool[Pooled??] 8 cigs for 1 mark. Soup, crout & macaroni for dinner. Sinton, Owen (Brynsienly) & Trevor left for Lager. Read "The Pilot of[at] Swan Creek" by Ralph Connor. Potatoe soup for supper.

Wed. 24th. Mashed cabbage, meat & soup for dinner. Servg beef for supper. Re'vd biscuits, about 17 small ones.

Thurs. 25th. Gave 3 biscuits for 3 cigs. Soup, fried potatoes and meat & gravy for dinner. Potatoes in skins & stinky cheese for supper. Doctor examined each patient. Told me I could ????& walk for an hour each day. Read "The Clean Heart" by A Sill Hutcherson.

Fri. 26th. Soup, macaroni & saurcrout for dinner. Saur crout with spuds in for supper. Got up in the evening.

Sat. 27th. Gave letter to Jerry Sgt. Ward swilled out. Soup, meat potatoes & gravy & blancmange for dinner. Porridge for supper. Read "Typhoon" by Joseph Conrad.

Sun. 28th. Rotten weather. Exchanged biscuit for cigarette. Exchanged 2 cobs of bread for 12 cigarettes. Meat & gravy, soup & fried potatoes for dinner. Crout with spuds in (not sour) for supper.

Mon .29th. Soup, tongue& gravy & sour crout for dinner. Stinky cheese & spuds in skins for supper. Sgt. came round from Lager & brot [brought?] us a cigarette each. I gave a piece of bread for 2 cigs.

Tues. 30 . Soup, cabbage & fried spuds for dinner. Read "The Golden Hope" by W. Clarke Russell. Jerry Sgt. came round for books for Eng. Officers going out of hospital. I hid mine in an empty bed as did a few others. Polalina for supper. Read "Penrod" by Booth Tarkington (H&S).

Wedn. 31st. Soup, meat & sour crout for dinner. Sour Crout with spuds in for supper. Exchanged cob of bread for 6 cigarettes & a piece of crust for for a little tobacco. Read "The Call of the City" by O. Henry. Got up after supper.

Aug 1st. Thurs. Read " Arsene Lupin" by Edgar Jepson & Maurice Leblanc. Meat & gravy, fried spuds & soup for dinner. Potatoe soup for supper. Some Englishman came into the ward from Ward7. Biscuits arrive. I sold 8 for 2 marks. Played solo in the evening.

Fri. 2nd. Soup, fried spuds & spinach for dinner. Gave a loaf for 4 cigs & 25 ph. Warrington left for the Lager. Gave 3 p.cs in. Semolina for supper. Smith got me 16 cigs for 2 marks.

Sat. 3rd. Read "For Charles The Rover" by May Wynne. Soup, meat & sour crout for dinner. Macaroni & jam for supper. Stayed in bed all day. Had some nasty pains in the stomach.

Sund. 4th. Red "The Truants" by AEW Mason. Soup, meat & gravy, macaroni & Blanc Mange for dinner. Veg. soup for supper. Stopped in bed all day.

Mond. 5th. Read "The House of Fortune" by -- - [he couldn't remember the author's name and I couldn't find it]. Soup, meat & stewed spuds for dinner. Crout & spuds for supper. Gave cob of bread for 6 cigarettes (1 to be brought in the morning). German military funeral. [This is almost certainly the one in the photographs on page 77].

Next is the following note which is an extract :

(from "The Truants")

Wounds gangrened.

Bin??el – Ghiramo to Ouargla.

"One must take one's risks."

"One wants to be needed by those one needs."

"A little may be a good thing but too much is enough."

Germany – Lazarett Lager Lechfeld – 6th-12th Aug (both inclusive)

1918

Aug 6th.Tues. Read "Lord Arthur Savile's Crime" & other prose pieces by Oscar Wilde. Soup, fried potatoes & cabbage for dinner. Military funeral (2 airmen). Macaroni & stewed fruit for supper. [It is possible that this is the funeral in the photograph also].

Wed. 7th. Soup, meat & gravy & macaroni for dinner. Sold a cob of bread for 1m & bot. 8 cigs for mark. Read "As in a Looking Glass" by ----[Again he hasn't entered the author but it is counted as a lost 1916 silent film directed by Frank Hall Crane and starring Kitty Gordon in her debut.]. Sour crout & spuds for supper.

Thurs. 8th. Borrowed 3 biscuits off Ward for bfat. Did not eat any bread. Soup, meat & stewed spuds for dinner. Potatoe soup for supper. Received conserve parcel & I box of biscuits between 2. Exchanged cocoa for 30 cigarettes. Sold 4 biscuits for one mark. Sold cob of bread for I mark. Gave 1 cigarette for biscuit. Had a shave & gave barber a biscuit. Sold 8 cigs for 1 mark. Bought 1 mark of cigarettes(8). Gave three biscuits for a long pipe to a Ruski.

Fri. 9th. Soup, macaroni & sour crout for dinner. Drew 1 tin of Bully, 1 sm tin of cheese, 1 sm tin of milk & a tin of dripping in the morning. Sold cob of bread for 1 mark. Semolina for supper. Had a bit of Plum Pudding off Ward. Played Bridge & Whist in the evening. Bo't. packet of writing paper & envelopes of[f?] the Sanitar[?] for 30 ph.

Sat. 10th. Sold cob of bread for 1 mark. Soup, meat & stewed spuds for dinner. Red "Our Flat" by R Andorn. Military funeral in the morning. Vegetable Soup for supper. Had some sport with mice in the evening about 11 o'c.

Sund. 11th. Sold cob of bread for 1 mark. Bo't. 7 cigarettes for 1 mark. Kelly sold tin of Bully for 4 marks. Soup, meat & gravy & macaroni for dinner. Limburger cheese for supper. Played bridge a'r tea. Sold tin of Bully for 4 marks. (2m Tyldesley).

Mon. 12th. Bo't 4 cigarettes, 2 marks. Dirty Dick put Watson thro' some massaging & gave him some gyp. Soup, tongue & sour crout for dinner. Played Bridge on the lawn. I got the grand slam. Had a shave, Ward lent me a pce of soap. Sgt. came round from the Lager & promised to send some conserves & biscuits. Potatoe soup for supper. Had a shave.

Germany – Lazarell-Lager Lechfeld – 1918 13th-20th Aug.[43]

Aug 13th. Tues. Bought 14 cigarettes for 2 marks. Soup, fried potatoes & cabbage for dinner. Macaroni & jam for tea. Read "The Scarlet Pimpernel" by Baroness Orczy. Ward gave Tyldesley & I a tin of Sardines between us.

Wed. 14th. Soup, meat & stewed spuds for dinner. Sour Crout & spuds for supper. Sold pckt. of tea for 4 marks(½ Tyldesley's). Sold tin of cheese for 3 marks. Bought ½ mark's worth of cigarettes. Drew biscuits & Blanc Mange.

Thurs. 15th. Soup, meat & gravy & fried spuds for dinner and Blanc Mange. Bought tin of herrings for 2 marks. Drew conserves, 1 pkt. Betn. 2[?]. Doctor examined all patients. Told me to get up all day. Limburger cheese & new spuds for supper.

Fri. 16th. Drew French Bully Beef. Changed tin of French cheese for tin of Beef. Exchanged beef for 30 cigarettes. Sold cob of bread for 1 mark. Soup,fried potatoes & cabbage for dinner. Got up after breakfast. Played Bridge. Macaroni & stewed fruit for supper. Mar[?]shed some cocoa in the evening.

Sat. 17th. Soup, kidney beans, meat & spuds for dinner. Read "The Cruise of the Snark" by Jack London. Vegetable soup for supper. Kept awake by an Irishman's (fm B'ham) jokes & carryings on. Sold 4 biscs. For 1 m to Ruski. Bought 8 cigs for 1 m.

Sund. 18 . Soup, macaroni, meat & gravy & Blanc Mange for dinner. Bought 12 cigs. for 2 m. Played crib in the morning. Cheese & potatoes for supper. Read "The Kidnapped President" by Guy Boothby. Dropped the draw of the locker in the evening & broke the glass of my watch & the swivel.

Mond. 19th. Soup, sour crout & meat for dinner. Vegetable soup for supper. Read "Happy Go Lucky" by Ian Hay. Had a hand of solo. Bo't 14 cigs for 2 m.

43 A new heading indicates that the following is on a new piece of paper.

Tues. 20th. Soup, fried spuds & cabbage for dinner. Got up about 7.30 & played Bridge from then until 8pm. Sold a tin of Bully for 3 marks. Semolina for supper.

Germany. – Lazarell Lager Lechfeld. – 1918-21st Aug – 27th Aug.

Aug 21st.Wed. Soup, kidney beans & spuds & meat for dinner. Played bridge in the afternoon. Read "The Sherrif of Dyke Hole" by Ridgwell Cullum. A Spaniard came round in the afternoon visiting accompanied by two officers & two interpreters(one a coloured South American). Sour crout & spuds for supper. Had a shave.

Thurs. 22nd. Soup, macaroni & meat & gravy for dinner. Lovely weather. Sat outside reading in the morning. Read "The Pillar of Light" by Louis Tracy. Vegetable soup for supper. Biscuits & conserves arrive. Jerry had to come three or four times to tell us to stop making a row. 3 cigs came down with biscuits for each man.

Fri. 23rd. Fried spuds & spinach for dinner. Cheese & spuds for supper. Read "The New Machiavelli" by H.G. Wells. Harriett, Kelly & Watson left the Lagarell [?] for Lager. Lovely weather. Played Bridge outside after tea. Sold cob of bread for 1m. Exchanged tea for 30 cigs & French bully beef for 30 cigs. (Tyldesly goes halves). Bo't 14 cigs for 2m & rec'd 5cigs off Jerry which he owed me.

Sat. 24th. Sold cob for 1m. Soup, kidney beans & spuds for dinner. Macaroni for supper. Had a lie down in the sun in the afternoon. Played Bridge after tea. Had a very interesting chat with Frisby of Yardley[44] about sport[?], waiters, hotels & other interesting people.

Sund. 25th. Sold cob for 1m. Weather breaks up. Soup, macaroni, meat & gravy for dinner. Cheese & spuds for supper. Played Bridge morning & afternoon. Blanc Mange for dinner[I think he means supper].

Mon. 26th. Soup, meat& gravy & beet-root for dinner. Spud soup for supper. Read "The House Opposite" by Rita. Felt bad in the evening.

44 Yardley is a suburb of South Birmingham.

Tues. 27th. Soup, macaroni & jam for dinner. Rob't Williams leaves Lagarell for Lager. Semolina for supper. Felt rotten in the evening, headache & sore throat. Moved from No. 23 bed to No. 11.

Germany. Lagarell-Lager Lechfeld. 28th Aug. 1918 – 1st Sept. 1918.

1918

Aug.28th. Wed. Did not feel well. Soup, meat& gravy& salad (lettuce & spuds) for dinner. Sour crout & spuds for supper. Read "A Cabinet Secret" by Guy Boothby. Played Bridge in the a'rnoon.

Thur. 29th. Soup, meat & sour crout for dinner. Pink crout for supper. Read "The Shulamite" by Alice & Claude Askew. Bought one marks worth of cigs(6). Have a bad cold & felt rotten.

Fri. 30th. Soup, macaroni & jam for dinner. Macaroni & stewed fruit for supper.

Sat. 31st. Soup, meat & stewed spuds for dinner. Visited No.1 Barrack. Sold a cob of bread to one of the lads for 1m. A wasp stung me in the right leg whilst I was in there. I knocked the same wasp down last night & it must have got into the trousers by somehow & having recovered it stung me. It fell on the floor when I pulled my trouser leg up & I killed it. Lloyd George[nickname?] put a bandage on the leg. B't 6 cigs 1m. B'ot a pipe & 2 cigs for 2m. Sour crout fot supper. Doctor came round in the evening & examined us all. I think the Sgt. & myself were marked for the Lager.

Sept. 1st. Sund. Soup, meat & gravy & lettuce for dinner. Cheese & spuds for supper. Bought 6 cigarettes for 1m. Visited No.1 barrack & had a chat with the lads.

Germany. Lagarell, Lager Lechfeld. 2nd Sept-7th Sept. 1918.

1918

Sept 2nd Mond. Soup, meat & potatoes for dinner. Conserves & biscuits arrive. Potatoe soup for supper. Played Bridge.

Tues. 3rd. Soup, macaroni & sourcrout for dinner. Semolina for supper. I went across to the cookhouse for manash[?] for the first time. Yorkey (Smelt) loses his reason & tries to get out of bed. Sgt. Wraith & Black & 3 others go to the Lager. Exchanged tea for 24 cigarettes. Sold cob for 1mark.

Wed. 4th. Got up for first time to wash floor. Sold cob for 1 mark.Soup, meat & sourcrout for dinner. Crout for supper.

Thurs. 5th. Soup, meat & gravy & fried potatoes for dinner. Crout for supper. Went to the kitchen with Barrington & peeled spuds. Had photographs taken. I bought 4. Exchanged tin of Bully for 28 cigs. [The photographs he refers to could be of the image in the small collection [19] but this is dated 1919 and doesn't name Barrington].

Fri. 6th. Soup, macaroni & jam for dinner. Sourcrout & macaroni for supper. Sold tin of Bully for 4m. Exchanged one for 26 cigs. Smelt of the Yorks is taken to an asylum. He was losing his reason first.

Sat. 7th. Had to scrub out the hut. Irish stew & soup for dinner. Read "Jane Eyre" by Charlotte Bronte.

Sept. 8th. Sund. Had a very weird dream last night that I had received a letter saying that mother was dead. Doctor caught me smoking in the ward & stopped my manash for 1 day. A fair had stopped somewhere near the hospital last night & we could hear the music & the noise distinctly. Meat & gravy, soup & fried spuds for dinner. Cheese & spuds for supper. Blanc Mange for dinner[?].

Mond. 9th. Read "Allan Quartermain" by Rider Haggard. Soup, meat& spuds for dinner. Macaroni & jam for supper.

Tues. 10th. Soup, potatoes & cabbage for dinner. Macaroni & sourcrout for supper. Sold bully for 3 marks.

There is no entry for 11th September 1918.

Sept 12 . Marked out at the Lagarell by the English Doctor.

Fri. 13th. Left the Lagarell & arrived at the Lager. Five of us went out, 1 Serbian, 1 Frenchman, 1 Ruski, 1 Italian & myself. Was searched at the office of the Lager & had my german money changed for lager money. [He hasn't used upper case letters]. Had a P.O. for 4/- taken from me, a cenysend[?], some French bullets & a tin of dripping.

Sat. 14th. Went to see the doctor in the morning at the Rivier. He marked me arb?? & fit for cernmunde?? Worked[He has crossed out this word for some reason] at the quan?? in the morning but did not do anything. Went with a party to empty spuds from a wagon at a siding into bogeys in the ?????[afternoon?].

Sund. 15th. Went to see the doctor again & he marked me lager arbide(light work). Did nothing all day.

Mon. 16th. Went to the N. C. O.'s camp & cleared the huts out in the morning. Went to the same camp in the afternoon & helped in the building of new huts.

Tues. 17th. Helped in the building of new huts at the NCO's camp morning & afternoon...

There is then a gap in the entries until:-

Sund. 15th Dec. 1918. Left Lager Lechfeld station at 12.15pm. Stayed on Augsburg station 3/4hr.
Stopped at Neusffingen. Stayed at Neu Ulm. Soup provided in a canteen but little partaken of. Brewed some cocoa in the same shanty. Left at 6.15pm. Next stop Ulm. Stopped at dns[???] station where Saddler had a rough argument with a Jerry. Went to sleep a'rwards.

Mond. 16th Dec. 1918. Woke up at 8am while the train was in Jinmending station. Went through W[E]engen [?]. Scenery very pretty. Arrived at Konstanz a'tr going round the lake at 10.25am. Changed trains and left

Konstanz at ????anbach. reinamshein[the text here is confusing because the last two words are written vertically on the edge of the page in his small note book at the rear where the diary picks up again by working back from the last page] 1.00pm. Passed through Berlingen. Stopped at Shaffhausen & rec'd cigs, postcards & flags. Passed thro' Rheinfall: very beautiful scenery. Stopped at Zurich. Rec'd apples, cigs, postcards & colours. Travelled down the side of the Rhein all the way. Stopped at Olten. Stopped at Berne. Very fine reception. Cigs & tobacco rec'd.

Passed the lake of Neuchatel. Arrived at the station of Neuchatel & had a tremendous welcome. Tobacco & chocolate etc. Arrived at Les Verrieres [?] (French) at 11.5pm. Very fine reception. Hot tea supplied. Between Neuchatel & Les Verrieres we crossed the Alps. Most magnificent scenery. 11.30pm arrived at "Pontarliers" (French). Magnificent reception; band played God Save the King, Marseilles & other selections. Rec'd café & Cognac. Bread & tinned meat. (Fireworks sent up just outside Neuchatel).

Tues. 17th Dec 1918. 8.15am. At Chaleris on the river Saone. Got out at St. Geruriain. Stayed at the camp until 4pm on the Thurs(19th). Khalsi issued to each man. Had a bath. Train left at 10.30pm 19th. Passed through Saincaize. Stopped at Nevers on the river Loire. Passed through Cosne & Borie.

Arrived at Amiens 11.30am 21st. Station very much knocked about. All the buildings round about the river Somme very much shattered. Passed thro' St. Roch & Pont Renny. Stopped at Abbeville some time. Stopped at Etaples & passed thro' Carniers. Stopped at Bouloygne & some of the RAMC staff got off to go on leave. Arrived at Calais & went to rest camp. I went down in reil[?] & car. Had cup of tea, bread & jam.

22nd. I went to bed at 4am. Rec'd 20 ????? ???? & ????.[45]

23rd. Left camp at 11.15am. Boat left Calais at 1.15pm. I was sea sick going across. (Crossed in the "Viper" – built at Govan Glasgow 1905). Arrived at Dover 2.5pm. Fine reception at Dover. Band played, ladies brought us tea & cakes, matches & p.cs & a parcel of tabacco, cigarettes, a pipe, flag & some toffee was presented to us on the way to the train. Left for Canterbury. Very mild reception. Attached to "B" Company, No.1

45 The words are smudged being at the very bottom of the page but it could be '...pay'.

Repatriation Camp. Many papers filled in including passes & ration tickets.

HMS Viper

24th. One party, resident in and near London, went home. Exchanged 20 marks German money for 10/-. Went to a concert in the E.F.C. in the evening.

25th. Rec'd kit in the morning & £2-10-0 pay. Had Christmas Dinner at the Camp. Went to see some pictures in E.F.C. in the evening. [Expeditionary Force Cinema].

26th. Left Canterbury stn. at 8.45am. Arrived London 11.15am. Left Willesden 12.30pm. Arr'd New St. 3.15pm. Left New St. 4.5pm. Arr'd home [Wolverhampton] 5.10pm.

This effectively ends his war diary but the note book also contains:

Accounts, Addresses, Letters/Postcards received and sent [both during the war and shortly after] and other diary entries of his days in the early weeks of the peace.

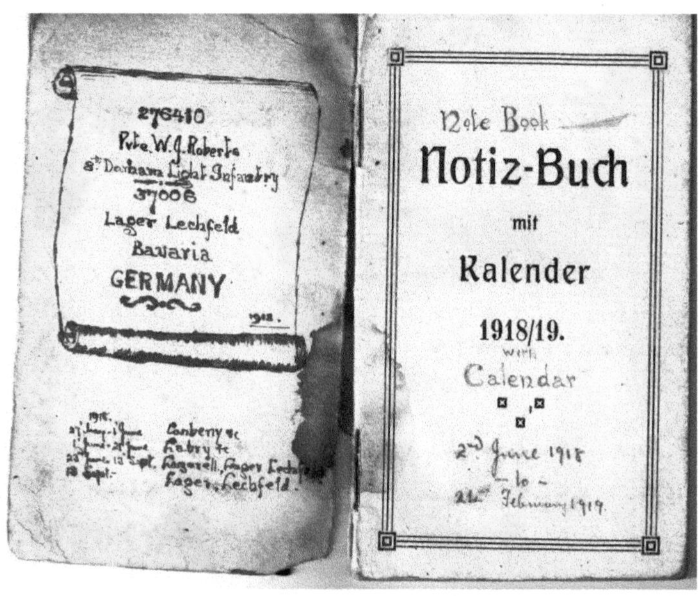

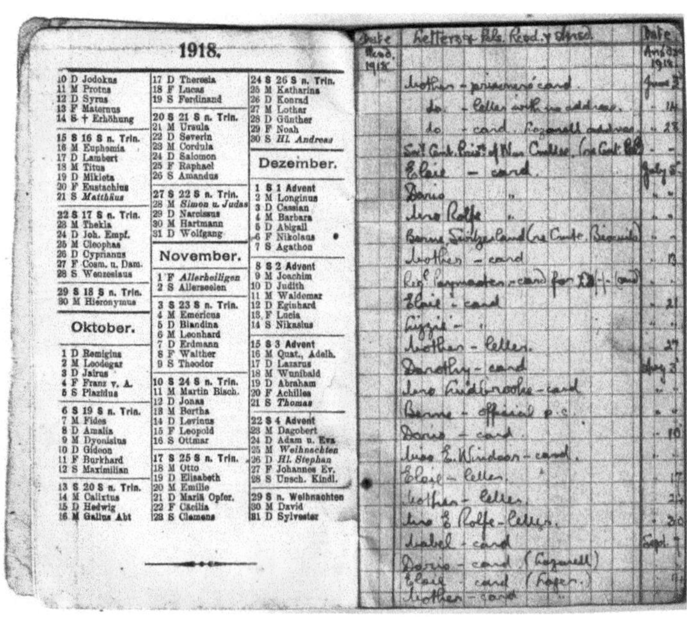

Rec'd.	Letters, Parcels &c.	Sent
1918 Sept. 17th	Biscuits, 1st Regt. from Berne. (no p.c.)	1918
	Lizzie – card.	Sept. 21
	Dorothy – card.	" "
	Mother – card.	" 29
	Mrs. E. Rolfe. – card.	" "
Oct. 1st	Biscuits. 20 lb. 13 Sept. 18. (52)	
" 9	Lizzie. letter (?) 9.8.18.	
" 10	Mrs. E. Rolfe. letter. 21.8.18	
" "	Biscuits. ? 28.9.18. (51?)	
	Mother. letter.	Oct. 10
	Mrs. E. Rolfe. card	" 13
" 19	Father. letter. 2.9.18.	
" 22	Lizzie. letter. 3.9.18.	
	Elsie – card	" 22
	Lizzie – card.	" 22
" 22	Regtl. Conserves 1st parcel (no p.c.)	
" 28	" " (do.)	
" "	" " (ack. 15th parcel) (no p.c.)	
" "	D.L.I. Cmte. Sunderland p.c.	30
Nov. 2nd	Regl. Biscuits	
	Berne p.c.	Nov. 7
	Doris (letter)	" 8
" 8	Regl. Conserves (no p.c.) no cigs	—
" 13	" " " 40 cigs	
" "	" " " 20 cigs	

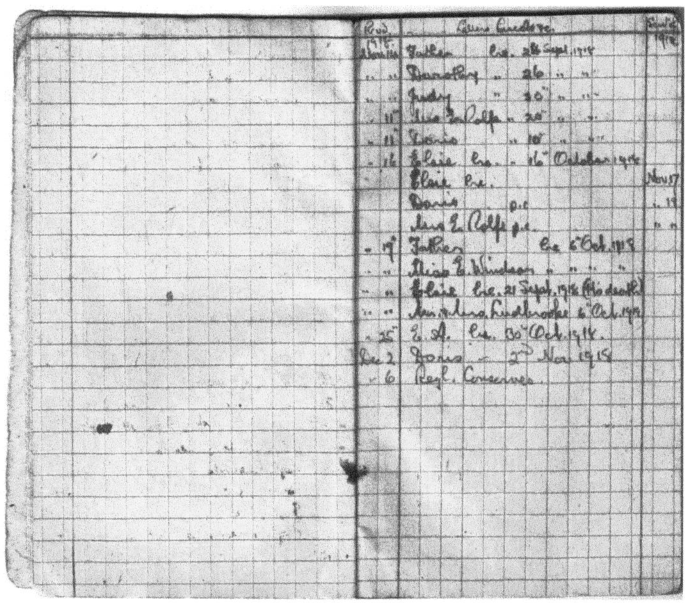

Rec'd.	Letters Cards &c.	Sent
1918 Nov. 11th	Father lre. 28 Sept. 1918	1918
" "	Dorothy " 26 " "	
" "	Judy " 30 " "	
" 11	Mrs E. Rolfe " 20 " "	
" 11	Doris " 10 " "	
" 16	Elsie lre. " 16th October 1918	
	Elsie lre.	Nov. 17
	Doris p.c.	" 19
	Mrs E. Rolfe p.c.	" "
" 19	Father lre 6th Oct. 1918	
" "	Miss E. Windsor " " "	
" "	Elsie lre. 21 Sept. 1918 (His death)	
" "	Mr & Mrs Lindbrooke 6th Oct. 1918	
" 25	E. A. lre. 30th Oct. 1918.	
Dec. 2	Doris – 2nd Nov. 1918	
" 6	Regl. Conserves.	

Date	Recd.	£	s	d
1918 Dec. 20	Camp Canterbury	2	10	-
22	" Calais 20 fr.		7	8
1919	" " "		7	8
Jan. 3	Regl. Paymaster cheque [illegible]	1	6	3
10	" " " [illegible]	1	6	3
	Cd. fwd.	5	17	10

Date	Exes.	s	d
1918 Dec. 29	Watch	14	6
·	Mother	6	·
30	Stamps	1	·
1919 Jan. 1	Papers & p. p cs.	2	·
·	Pictures (& 29th Dec.) [illegible] (3)	2	·
3	Mother	6	·
·	Pictures & stamps	1	6
4	Pens (Wm.) & papers (1/10)	2	·
6	Pictures	1	3
9	Pictures	1	3
10	Mother	10	·
·	[illegible]	8	·
·	The Royal Pants	1	10
11	Pictures (Victoria St.)	1	·
·	Mother	2	·
12	Chapel (collection)	·	3
13	Pictures – Queens	1	3
14	" – Victoria St.	1	·
·	Cigarettes (5½)	·	6
13	Confectionery &c.	2	7
15	Mother & Freddie	1	3
·	Pictures – Agricl. Hall	1	3
16	Stamps	1	·
·	Pictures – Qns.	1	3
	Cd. fwd.	3	12 8

Date	Letters &c. sent off. – Calls made.
Dec. 27	Mrs. Hunt. (letter.)
28	Pictures (Wm. Queens)
30	Winnie (letter & p.c. [illegible])
·	Ethel (p.c. [illegible])
·	Mrs. E. Rolfe (letter.)
1919 Jan. 1	Reg. Paymaster re credits & D. R. p.o.
·	Pictures (Queens Wm.)
2	Mathieson – ltr. & 4 pcs.
3	Mabel – ltr.
·	Harold Brown – p.c.
·	A. Taylor – p.c.
·	Regl. Paymaster. – ltr. re diff. in pay. [illegible]
·	Pictures (Queens Wm.)
4	R.P.B. Williams – p.c.
·	J.B. Dixon, H.Sec., P.O.W. Fund, B'm. – ltr.
6	Pictures (Queen's Wm.)
7	Library Wm.
·	Mrs. Godfrey – ltr. & 2 photos not Regd.
8	Library Wm.
9	[illegible]
·	Pictures (Queens Wm.)
10	The Royal pants Red Riding Hood.
·	Pictures (Victoria St.)
11	Chapel (Queen St. Congregational).
14	Doris – ltr.

Date	Letters &c. recd. – Calls recd.
Dec. 29	Mabel called
1919 Jan. 1	Mathieson – ltr. & p.c.
3	Harold Browne – p.c.
·	Mrs. Rolfe – ltr.
·	Regl. Paymaster – cheq. 1-6-3.
·	Mabel – ltr.
6	Mrs. E. Godfrey ([illegible]) Regd. ltr.
7	A. Taylor – p.c.
·	R.P.B. Williams – p.c.
11	Reg. Paymr. – cheque £1-6-3.
·	Miss Davis called & left card for [illegible]
14	Winnie – ltr.
·	Harold Browne – ltr.
16	Doris – ltr.
18	Reg. Paymr. – cheque £1-6-3 [illegible]
·	Mrs. Rolfe – ltr. [illegible]
·	B'm. R. P.O.W. Cttee. – invitn. card for [illegible]
·	W. Gordon – p.c.
?	Freddie Richardson – ltr.
?	R.P.B. Williams – ltr.
?	Norah Steele. – ltr.
26	Recd. cheq. £2.12.6 Regl. Pr. 4 & 5th week.

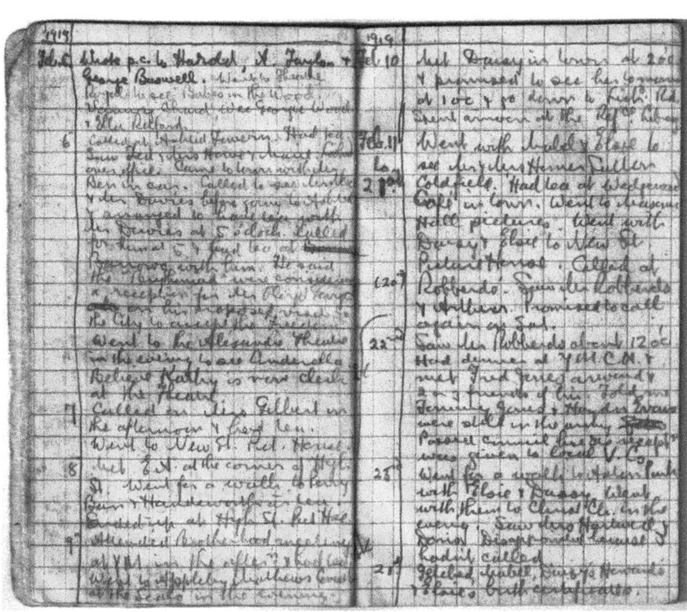

3d. 24" Went to Mitchells with letter from Mr. Taylor for Mrs Hunt. Saw Mrs Mitchell. Took Mrs Hunt to sign papers at Victoria Rd. Police Station re Heward (Eligibility Form & Pension Form). Posted Eligibility Form to Paymaster Blackheath & wrote ltr. to him re Heward's credits. Posted Pension Form & Birth Certs to [illegible] Cornwell [illegible].
Caught 8.10 train for [illegible] Hill – Called on Dr Rhodes Dudley Rd. & got bottle of medicine & tablets. He advised me to report sick at War hospital. Mother said Dr. had given up all hopes of Idwal pulling through.

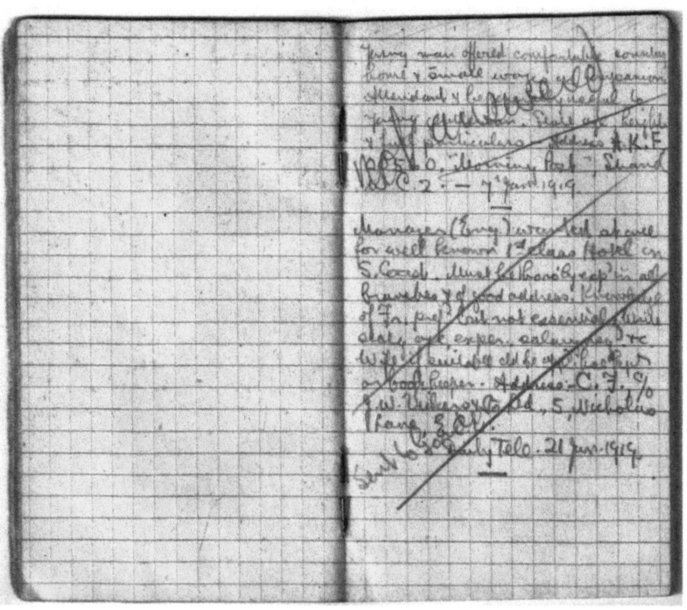
Young man offered comfortable country home & small wage [illegible] Attendant & [illegible] useful to young [illegible]. State age, height & full particulars – Address A.K.F. 560, "Morning Post", Strand W.C.2. – 7th Jan 1919.

Manager (Eng.) wanted at once for well known 1st class Hotel on S. Coast. Must be thoro'ly exp'd in all branches & of good address. Knowledge of Fr. pref'd but not essential. Write state age, exper. salary req'd &c. Wife if available cld be empl'd [illegible] as bookkeeper. Address:- C. J. c/o J. W. Vickers & Co Ltd., 5, Nicholas Lane, E.C.
Sent to [illegible] Daily Telg. 21 Jan 1919.

There is then an address book :

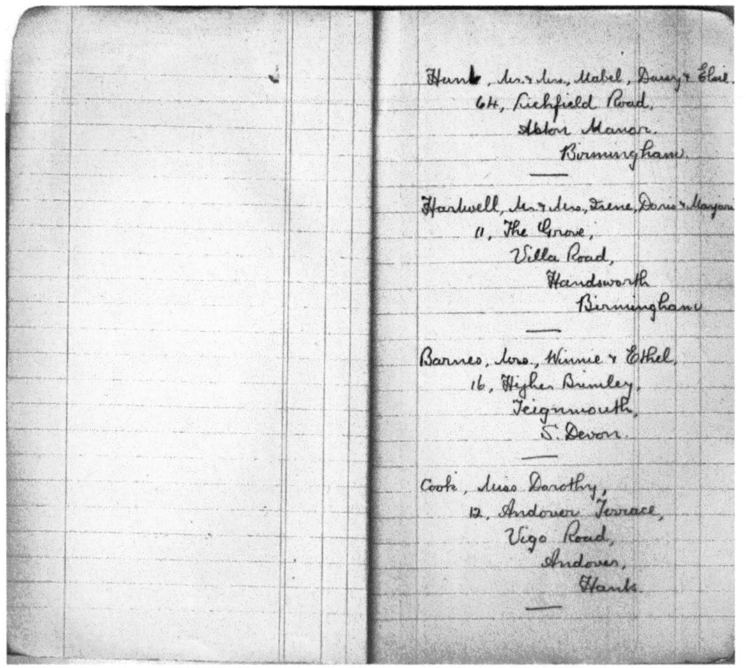

Hunt, Mr. & Mrs., Mabel, Daisy & Elsie.
64, Lichfield Road,
Aston Manor.
Birmingham.

—

Hartwell, Mr. & Mrs., Irene, Doris & Marjori
11, The Grove,
Villa Road,
Handsworth
Birmingham

—

Barnes, Mrs., Winnie & Ethel,
16, Higher Brimley,
Teignmouth,
S. Devon.

—

Cook, Miss Dorothy,
12, Andover Terrace,
Vigo Road,
Andover,
Hants.

—

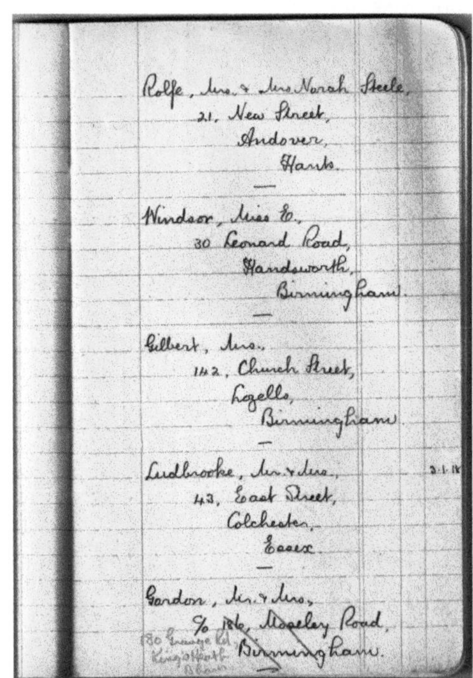

Rolfe, Mrs. & Mrs Norah Steele,
21, New Street,
Andover,
Hants.

—

Windsor, Miss E.
30 Leonard Road,
Handsworth,
Birmingham.

—

Gilbert, Mrs.
142, Church Street,
Lozells,
Birmingham.

—

Ludbrooke, Mr. & Mrs. 3.1.18
43, East Street,
Colchester,
Essex.

—

Gordon, Mr. & Mrs.
c/o 186, Moseley Road,
Birmingham.

Howe, Mr & Mrs. Ted,
"Ashted Tavern"
28, Henry Street,
Ashted,
Birmingham

—

Kelsey, Mr. Ben G.,
227, Hagley Road,
Edgbaston,
Birmingham

—

Kelsey, Mr. Geo. S., (Senior)
"Elsinore",
Water Orton,
Nr. B'ham

—

Woodward, Mr. J.,
86, Summer Road,
Edgbaston,
Birmingham

—

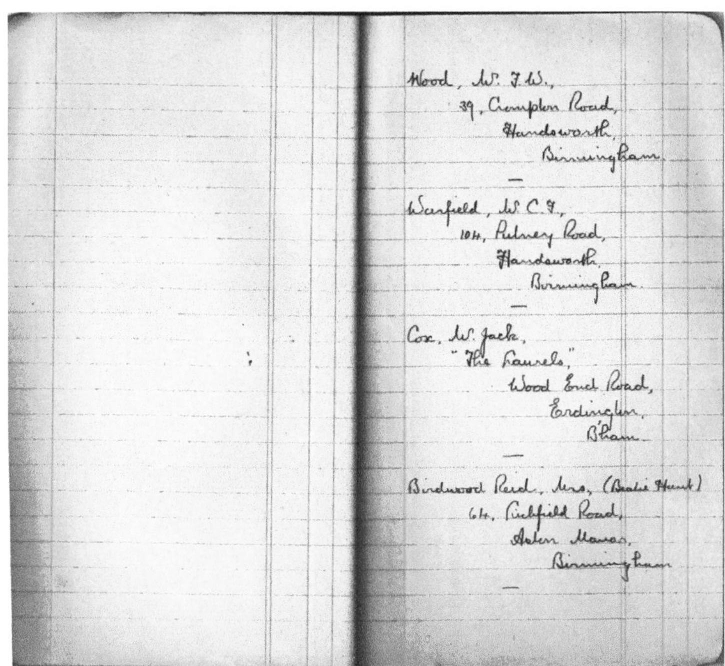

Wood, Mr. F.W.,
39, Crompton Road,
Handsworth,
Birmingham

—

Warfield, Mr C.F.,
104, Putney Road,
Handsworth,
Birmingham

—

Cox, Mr. Jack,
"The Laurels,"
Wood End Road,
Erdington,
B'ham

—

Birdwood Reid, Mrs, (Bessie Hunt)
64, Birchfield Road,
Aston Manor,
Birmingham

—

Hank, Mr. & Mrs., Mabel, Daisy & Elsie.
64, Lichfield Road,
Aston Manor.
Birmingham.

—

Hartwell, Mr. & Mrs., Irene, Doris & Marjorie
11, The Grove,
Villa Road,
Handsworth
Birmingham

—

Barnes, Mrs., Winnie & Ethel,
16, Higher Bumley,
Teignmouth,
S. Devon.

—

Cook, Miss Dorothy,
12, Andover Terrace,
Vigo Road,
Andover,
Hants.

—

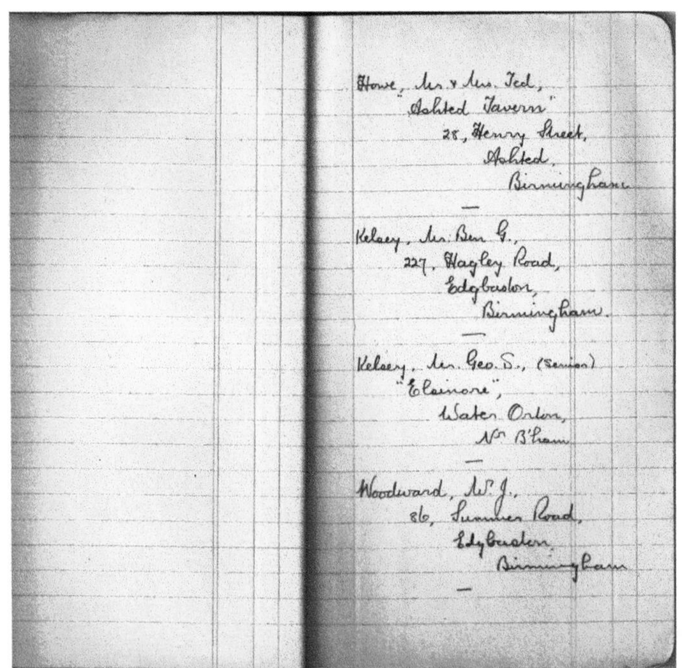

Howe, Mr. & Mrs. Ted,
"Ashted Tavern"
28, Henry Street,
Ashted,
Birmingham

—

Kelsey, Mr. Ben G.,
227, Hagley Road,
Edgbaston,
Birmingham.

—

Kelsey, Mr. Geo. S., (Senior)
"Elsinore",
Water Orton,
Nr. B'ham

—

Woodward, W. J.,
86, Summer Road,
Edgbaston,
Birmingham

—

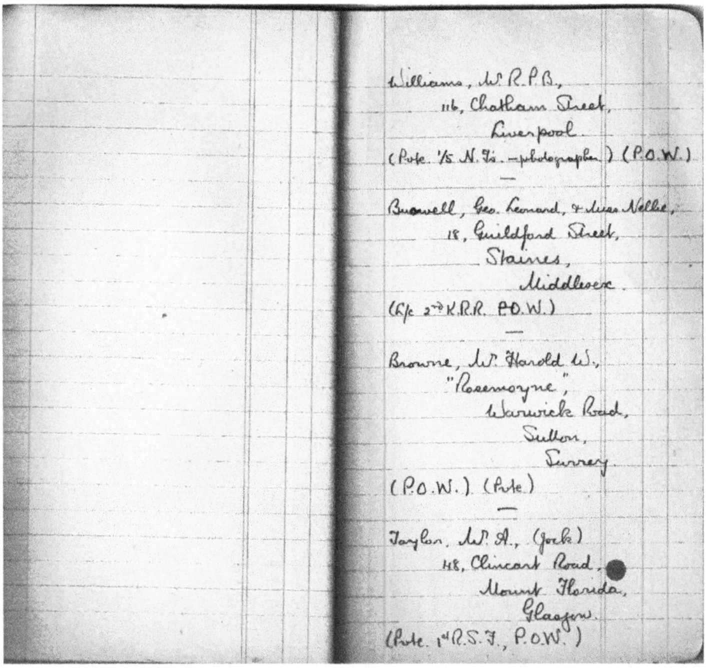

Williams, Mr R.P.B.,
116, Chatham Street,
Liverpool.
(Pte. 1/5 N. Fs. – photographer) (P.O.W.)

—

Burwell, Geo. Leonard, & Miss Nellie,
18, Guildford Street,
Staines,
Middlesex.
(L/c 2nd K.R.R. P.O.W.)

—

Browne, Mr Harold W.,
"Rosemoyne",
Warwick Road,
Sutton,
Surrey.
(P.O.W.) (Pte.)

—

Taylor, Mr A., (Jock)
48, Clincart Road,
Mount Florida,
Glasgow.
(Pte. 1st R.S.F., P.O.W.)

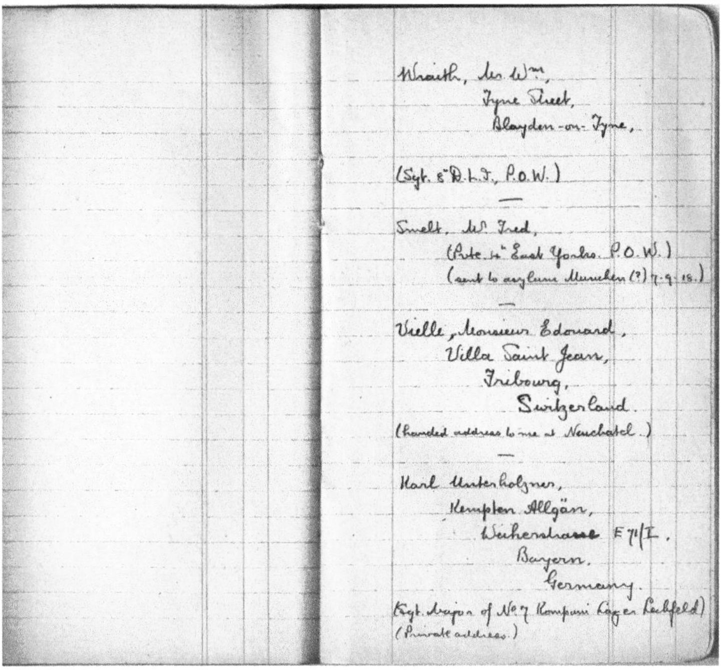

Wraith, Mr Wm,
Tyne Street,
Blaydon-on-Tyne,

(Sgt. 8th D.L.I., P.O.W.)

—

Smelt, Mr Fred,
(Pte. 4th East Yorks. P.O.W.)
(sent to asylum Munchen (?) 7.9.18.)

—

Vielle, Monsieur Edouard,
Villa Saint Jean,
Fribourg,
Switzerland.
(handed address to me at Neuchatel.)

—

Karl Unterholzner,
Kempten Allgäu,
Weiherstrasse E 71/I.
Bayern,
Germany.
(Sgt. Major of No 7 Kompani Lager Lechfeld)
(Private address.)

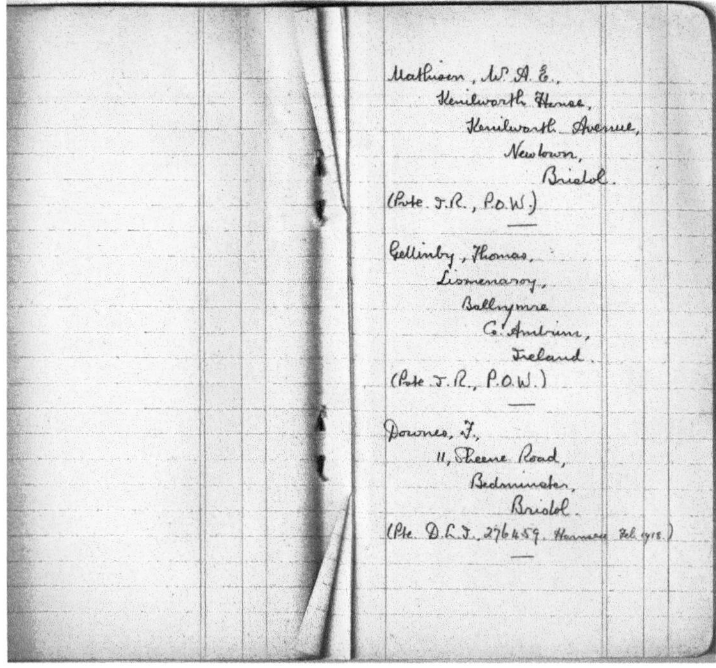

Mathison, Mr. A. E.,
Kenilworth House,
Kenilworth Avenue,
Newtown,
Bristol.
(Pte. J.R., P.O.W.)
—
Gellinby, Thomas,
Lismenaroy,
Ballymure
Co. Antrim,
Ireland.
(Pte. J.R., P.O.W.)
—
Downes, F.,
11, Sheene Road,
Bedminster,
Bristol.
(Pte. D.L.I. 276459. Harness Feb. 1918.)
—

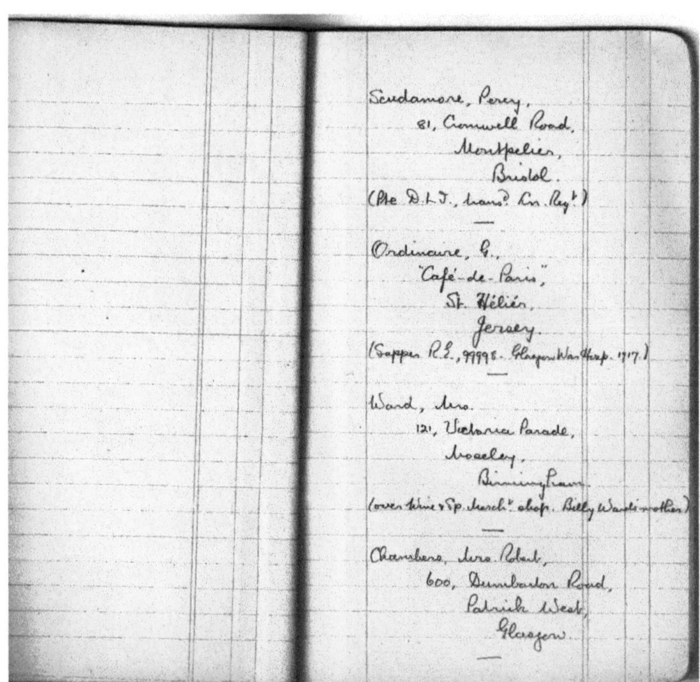

Scudamore, Percy,
81, Cromwell Road,
Montpelier,
Bristol.
(Pte D.L.I., trans^d^ Lin. Reg^t^)
—
Ordinaire, E.,
"Café-de-Paris",
St. Heliér,
Jersey.
(Sapper R.E., 99998. Glasgow War Hosp. 1917.)
—
Ward, Mrs.
121, Victoria Parade,
Moseley,
Birmingham.
(over Wine & Sp. Merch^t^ shop. Billy Ward's mother)
—
Chambers, Mrs Robert,
600, Dumbarton Road,
Partick West,
Glasgow.
—

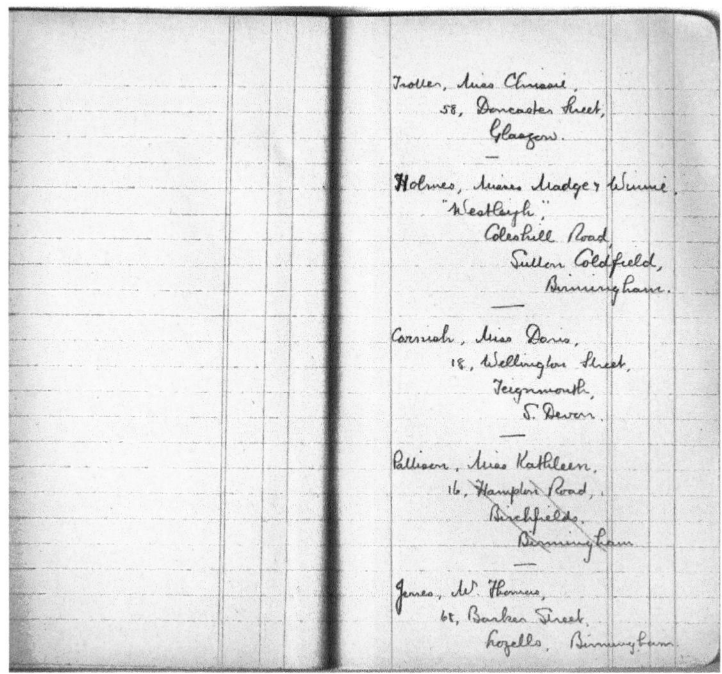

Trotter, Miss Chrissie,
58, Doncaster Street,
Glasgow.

—

Holmes, Misses Madge & Winnie,
"Westleigh,"
Coleshill Road,
Sutton Coldfield,
Birmingham.

—

Cornish, Miss Doris,
18, Wellington Street,
Teignmouth,
S. Devon.

—

Pallison, Miss Kathleen,
16, ~~Hampton Road,~~
~~Birchfields,~~
~~Birmingham.~~

—

Jones, Mr. Thomas,
68, Barker Street,
Lozells, Birmingham

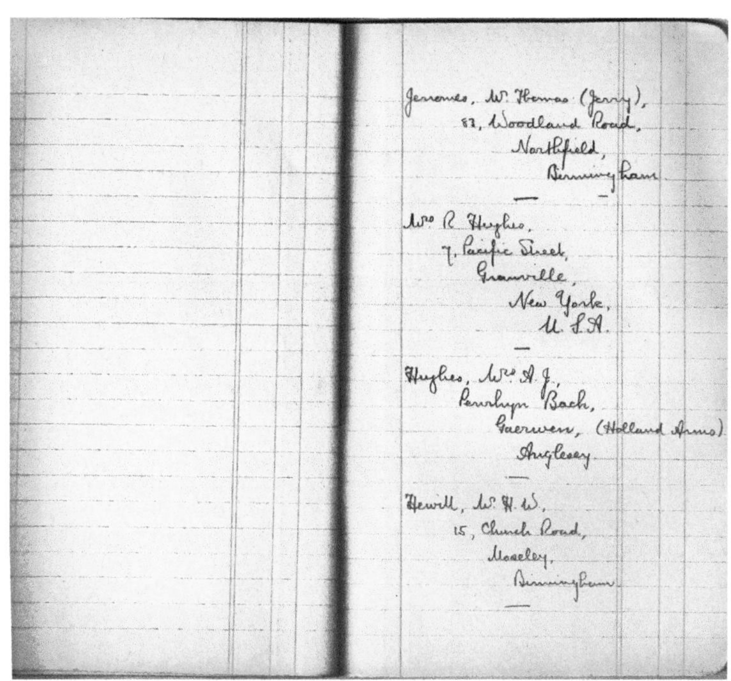

Jeromes, Mr. Thomas (Jerry),
83, Woodland Road,
Northfield,
Birmingham

—

Mrs R. Hughes,
7, Pacific Street,
Granville,
New York,
U.S.A.

—

Hughes, Mrs. A. J.,
Penrhyn Bach,
Gaerwen, (Holland Arms)
Anglesey.

—

Hewitt, Mr. H. W.,
15, Church Road,
Moseley,
Birmingham

—

~~Hobard~~
Hobart, Mrs J.W. (Doris Cornish's sister)
"Cartlee",
Balmoral Road,
St. Andrews,
Bristol.
—
Reid, Mrs Birdwood
c/o Miss Johnson,
64, Zoar Street,
Morley,
Leeds. (Temp. address)
—
Barnes, Misses Ethel & Winnie,
15, Alexander Square,
South Kensington,
London S.W.3. (Temp. add)
—
The Regimental Paymaster,
No 2 (D.L.I.)
York
—

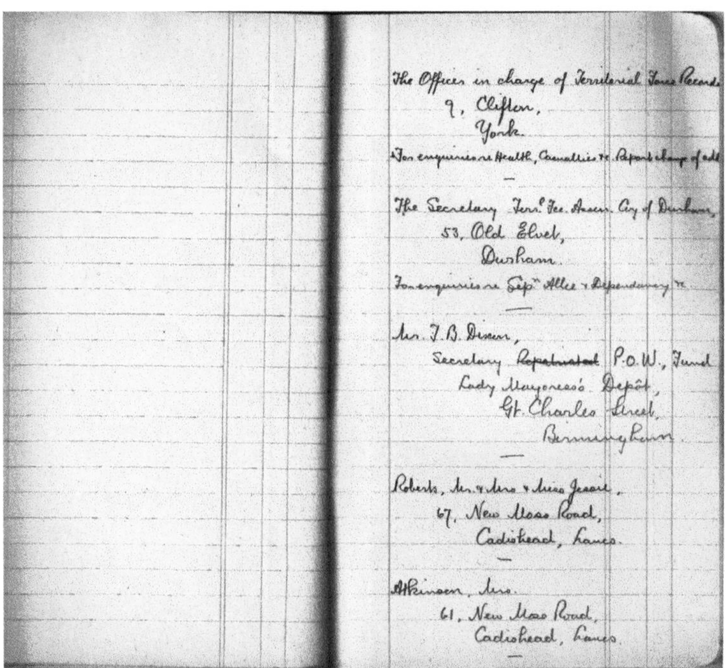

The Officer in charge of Territorial Force Records
9, Clifton,
York.
*For enquiries re Health, Casualties &c. Report change of add
—
The Secretary Terr. Fce. Assn. Cty of Durham,
53, Old Elvet,
Durham.
For enquiries re Sepn Allce & Dependency &c
—
Mr T.B. Dixon,
Secretary ~~Repatriated~~ P.O.W. Fund
Lady Mayoress's Depôt,
Gt. Charles Street,
Birmingham.
—
Roberts, Mr & Mrs & Miss Jessie,
67, New Moss Road,
Cadishead, Lancs.
—
Atkinson, Mrs.
61, New Moss Road,
Cadishead, Lancs.
—

Rollinson, Mr Jack & Harrie,
57, New Moss Road,
Cadishead, Lancs.
—
Roberts, Mr John Richard & Mrs Lizzie,
Irlam,
Manchester.
—
Babbington, Mr Wm & Mrs Jinnie,
Cadishead, Lancs
—
Edwards, Mr Arthur Llewelyn,
"Glaslyn"
Penrhosgarnedd,
Bangor.
—
Hughes, Mr Griffiths,
"Bellmount",
Penrhosgarnedd,
Bangor
—

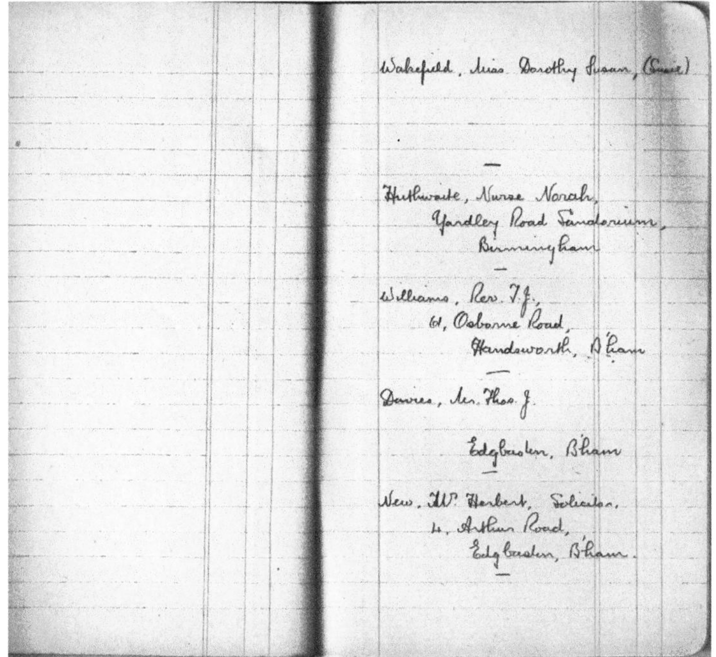

Wakefield, Miss Dorothy Susan, (Susie)
—
Huthwaite, Nurse Norah,
Yardley Road Sanatorium,
Birmingham
—
Williams, Rev. T.J.,
61, Osborne Road,
Handsworth, B'ham
—
Davies, Mr Thos J.
Edgbaston, B'ham
—
New, W. Herbert, Solicitor,
4, Arthur Road,
Edgbaston, B'ham.
—

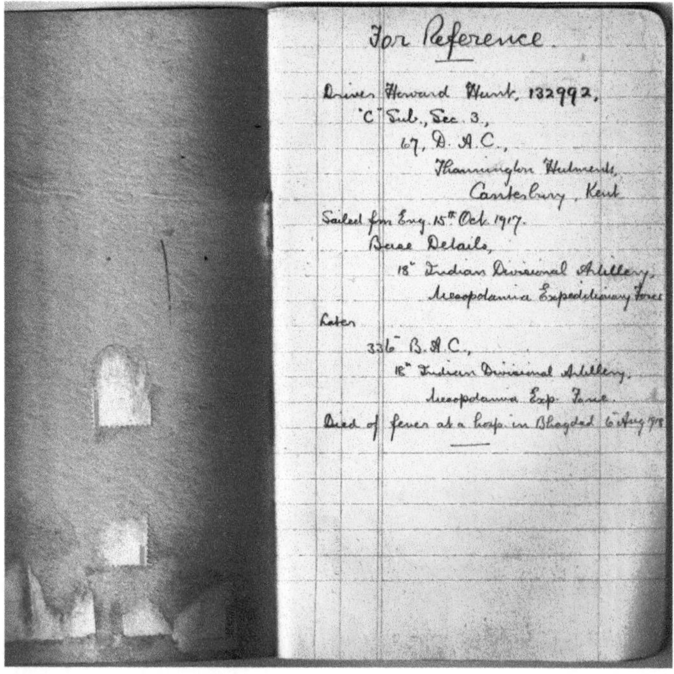

For Reference.

Driver Howard Hunt, 132992,
"C" Sub., Sec. 3,
67. D.A.C.,
Thannington Hutments,
Canterbury, Kent

Sailed from Eng. 15th Oct. 1917.
Base Details,
18th Indian Divisional Artillery,
Mesopotamia Expeditionary Force

Later
336th B.A.C.,
18th Indian Divisional Artillery,
Mesopotamia Exp. Force.

Died of fever at a hosp. in Baghdad 6th Aug 1918

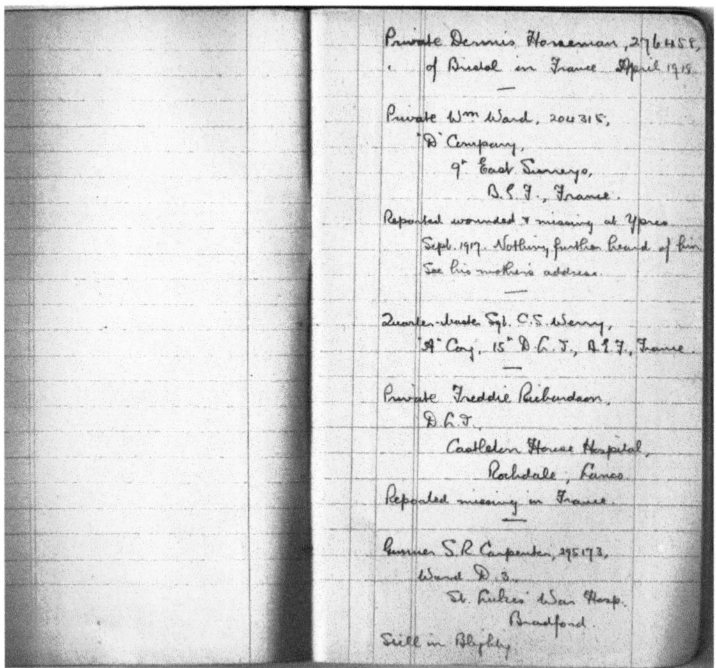

Private Dennis Horseman, 276458,
of Bristol in France April 1918.

Private Wm Ward, 204318,
"D" Company,
9th East Surreys,
B.E.F., France.
Reported wounded & missing at Ypres
Sept. 1917. Nothing further heard of him
See his mother's address.

Quarter-Master Sgt. C.S. Werry,
"A" Coy, 15th D.L.I., B.E.F., France.

Private Freddie Richardson,
D.L.I.,
Castleton House Hospital,
Rochdale, Lancs.
Reported missing in France.

Gunner S.R. Carpenter, 295173,
Ward D.3.
St. Luke's War Hosp.
Bradford.
Still in Blighty

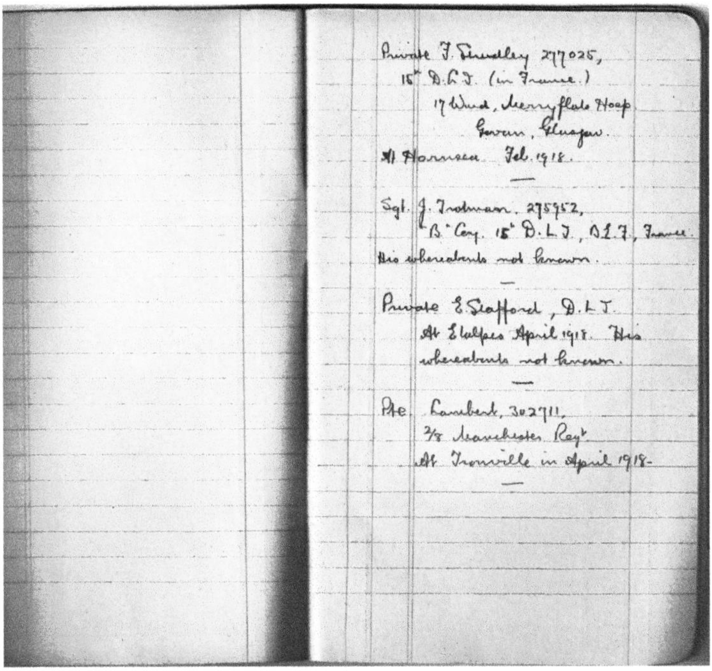

Private F. Tweedley 277025,
15th D.L.I. (in France.)
17 Ward, Merryflats Hosp.
Govan, Glasgow.
At Hornsea Feb. 1918.

—

Sgt. J. Trotman. 275952,
"B" Coy. 15th D.L.I., B.E.F., France.
His whereabouts not known.

—

Private E. Stafford, D.L.I.
At Etaples April 1918. His
whereabouts not known.

—

Pte. Lambert, 302711,
2/8 Manchester Regt.
At Trouville in April 1918.

—

Next follows a letter from one of the sisters of Thorpe who died in the next bed to my father in hospital in Germany during the night of 6th-7th June 1918.

Recd 6 Jun '19

61 Wharton St,
North Skelton
In Cleveland
Yorks.

To. 276410
Pte W. J. Roberts.

Dear Sir

This morning we have received the information from the Red Cross that you are able to give us news of my brother.

I am Registering you two Photos of my Brother. & I would be grateful if you could let us know if it is the same boy as the one whom you saw die in Limberg

If it is the same would you be so kind

kind

as give us all Particulars it is Possible

I am registering Photo to you & would thankful if you would Register them back, as they are Precious to & me, being all I have.

If it is at all Possible will you let us know how he was operated upon & if he suffered in any way.

We are very sorry to trouble about these things: for I know you will ~~be~~ only two unwilling to have the horrors you have undergone & seen, brought

brought

back to your memory. But I offer you my heartiest congratulations on your being lucky enough to get back to your Parents home & comfort.

Thanking you in anticipation for any information you can give us, of the one who was very dear to us, (being our baby brother)

I remain
Sincerely Yours

Mrs. E. Godfrey.

On behalf of my mother Mrs E. E. Thorpe who is ill from the sad news received this morning.

The last document is a receipt for the registration of my father's reply on 7th January 1919, the day after having received it.

Regn. No. H1 Certificate of Posting of a Registered Postal Packet

A Postal Packet addressed as under, upon which a Fee of Two Pence has been paid, in addition to the Postage {of ...... s. ...... d.} {for Parcels only.} has been registered and posted here this day:—

Date Stamp

WOLVERHAMPTON · DUDLEY-R? · P · JA · 19

Accepting Officer's Signature (or Initials)

THE LETTERS

I set out below letters received by my father from comrades with whom he fought in Flanders and France and was later taken prisoner to Germany. However, before these are replies to him from the authorities to apparent requests to be placed elsewhere in the armed forces while he was in hospital given that there are references to "Sick Berth".

1. From the Royal Marines, 6th December 1915.

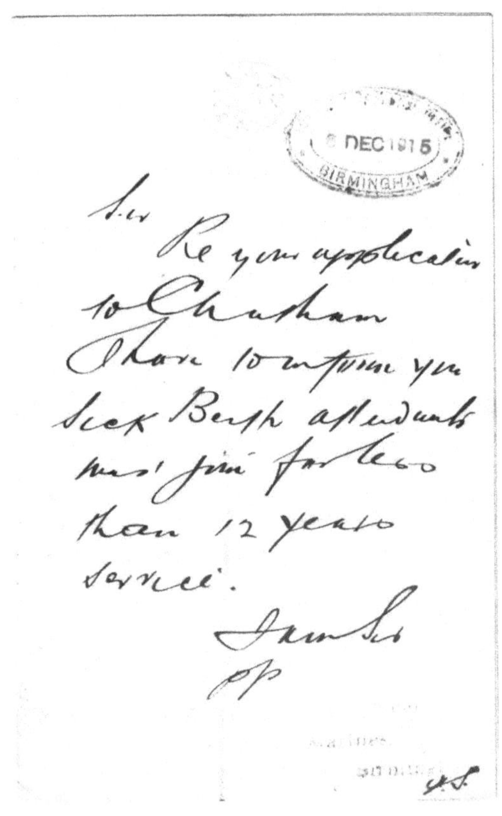

6 DEC 1915
BIRMINGHAM

Sir

Re your application to Chatham I have to inform you Sick Berth attendants must join for less than 12 years service.

I am Sir

2. Letter from Surgeon General, 6 December 1915.

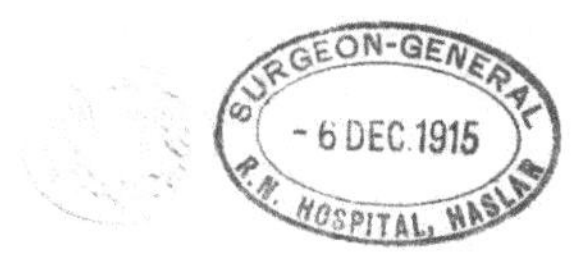

Dear Sir

In reply to your letter of the 2nd inst I am directed by the Surgeon General to say that no Sick Berth Ratings are being entered for the period of the war—

Your testimonials returned herewith.

Yours faithfully

Wm R.P. Hobbs

Secretary

3. Letter from John Williams in Anglesey.

Dec. 18th/15

Dear Sir,

I have just returned from the Kinmel Park today, and understand that an R.A.M.C. Corps is likely to be formed there, in the near future. This will be made known through the medium of the Welsh Press, & of the English papers circulating in Wales.

Kind regards

Yours faithfully

John Williams

4. PC from Billy Ward.

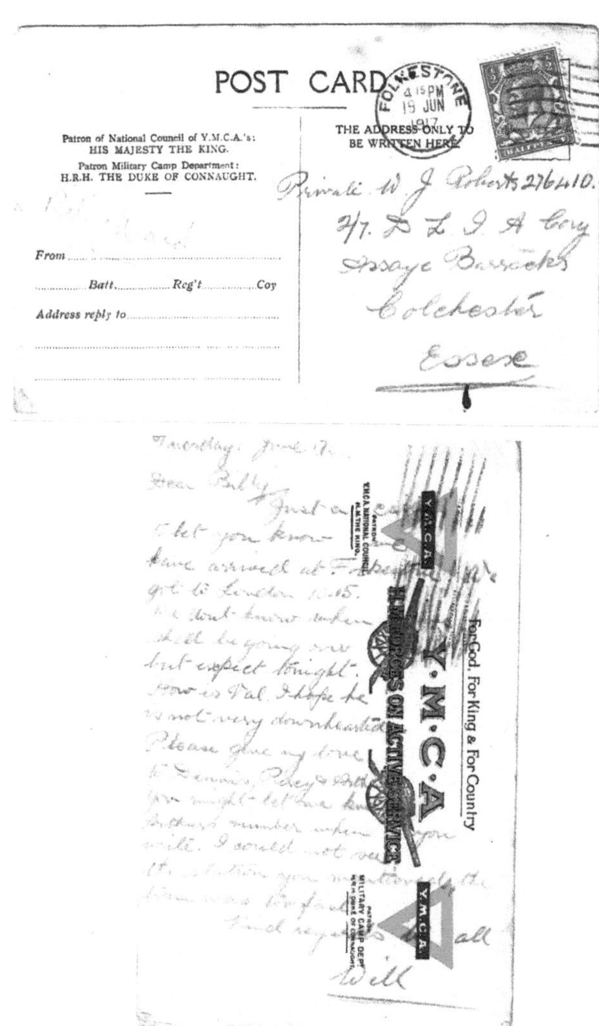

POST CARD

Patron of National Council of Y.M.C.A.'s:
HIS MAJESTY THE KING.
Patron Military Camp Department:
H.R.H. THE DUKE OF CONNAUGHT.

From ....
.... Batt. .... Reg't .... Coy
Address reply to ....

THE ADDRESS ONLY TO BE WRITTEN HERE

FOLKESTONE 4.15 PM 19 JUN 1917

Private W J Roberts 276410.
2/7. D L I A Coy
Assaye Barracks
Colchester
Essex

Tuesday June 19

Dear Billy
Just a card [illegible]
to let you know [illegible]
have arrived at Folkestone. We
got to London 10.15.
We don't know when
shall be going over
but expect tonight.
How is Val. I hope he
is not very downhearted.
Please give my love
to Dennis, Percy & [illegible]
You might let me know
Arthur's number when you
write. I could not see
the station you mentioned, the
time was too short.
Kind regards to all
Will

5. PC from Val Filey [Tiley?]

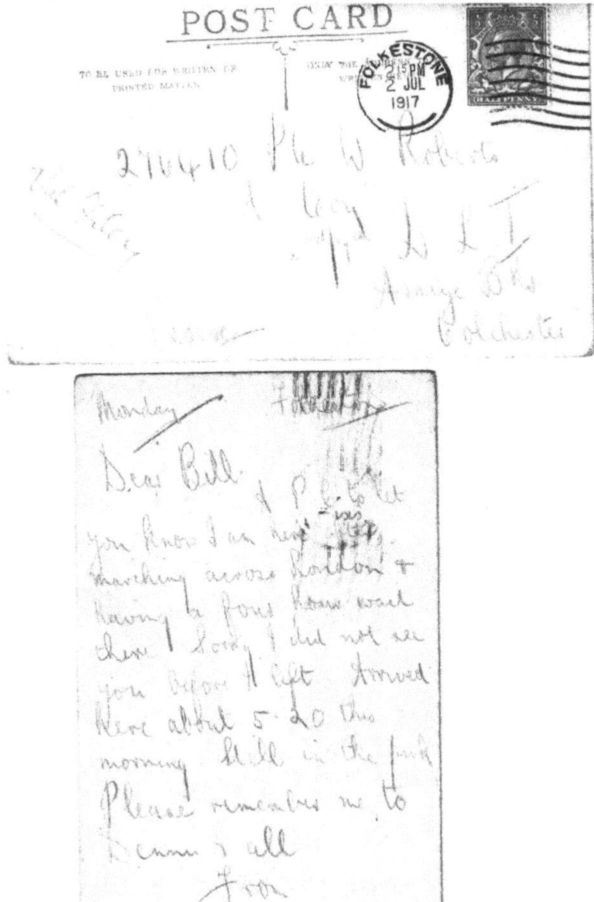

POST CARD

FOLKESTONE
2.15 PM
2 JUL
1917

274410 Pte W Roberts
1 Coy
4th L R T
Arrays Bks
Colchester

Monday

Dear Bill
A P.C. to let you know I am here after marching across London & having a four hours wait there. Sorry I did not see you before I left. Arrived here about 5.20 this morning. Still in the pink. Please remember me to Dennis & all.
From
Yours
Val

Post card from Billy Ward. [This could be out of sequence as it wishes him well, possibly when he was in either in hospital or POW camp.]

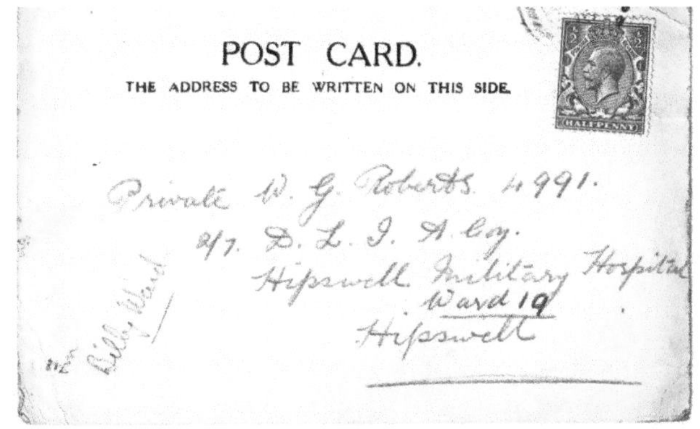

POST CARD.

THE ADDRESS TO BE WRITTEN ON THIS SIDE.

Private W. G. Roberts 4991.
2/7. D.L.I. A. Coy.
Hipswell Military Hospital
Ward 19
Hipswell

Billy Ward

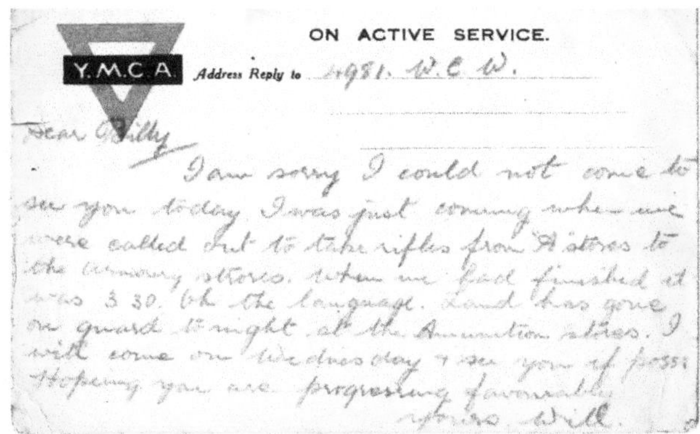

ON ACTIVE SERVICE.

Y.M.C.A. Address Reply to 4981. W.C.W.

Dear Billy

I am sorry I could not come to see you today I was just coming when we were called out to take rifles from A stores to the Armoury stores. When we had finished it was 3.30. Oh the language. Land has gone on guard to night at the Ammunition stores. I will come on Wednesday & see you if possi[ble]
Hoping you are progressing favourably
Yours Will.

Note from WR Stephens [undated].

This could be out of sequence because it mentions the recovery of private Roberts.

This could be from either of the serious wounds he received in the two significant battles in which he fought or during the world wide 'flu epidemic which occurred at the time of WW1.

Dear Roberts,
Thanks for your letter. We are delighted to hear you are making good progress, & hope it will continue. Am sending Tea & Sugar & Eggs & Writing Paper. I am awfully sorry that I cannot get round myself to-day. All send Best wishes. Shall try to come round on ~~[illegible]~~ Sunday. My love to Nursie.

Yours truly
W R Stephens

Am telling Bearer to wait for Dirty Linen. Can you send it out.

Post card from Ralph Byron Gordon. 17th Jan 1919.

POST CARD

Mr W. J. G. Roberts,
45 Johnson Street,
Blakenhall,
Wolverhampton.

186 Moseley Road
B'ham 17th Jan 1919.

Dear Mr Roberts,
Quite a pleasant surprise to receive your letter. Can you come on Sunday for tea say about 4 o'c? if not one evening about 7.30 to 8. Write per return if you can manage Sunday, so that we shall know if to expect you. All news later. Kind regards from both
Ralph Byron Gordon

Letter from Dennis [Houseman?] 23.9.17 in Colchester.

Colchester
23.9.17.

Dear Billy

I was jolly glad to get your letter, for I was beginning to wonder where you had got to. I'm sorry to tell you poor Billy Ward has been killed & so have Val Siley & Goddard. Harry Howard is a prisoner in Germany. Your mother sent me a nice little letter & also packet of cigarettes & it was most kind of her I must write & thank her for it. Gosling wrote me this week he is quite well & wished to be remembered to you. Joe leaves the battalion next month for his senior officers course he will not be coming back 3 of them are going Major Page, Capt Bowman & Joe & they will all be going to France when they have finished whether I shall go with him I don't know if I do it will probably mean going to France with him, for myself I don't mind much but I'm afraid mother would not be able to stand it, of course it would be practically the end of January before I got out there. I am glad to hear you are in a decent lot & getting better food, your hut must be a miniature "black hole of

Calcutta" there is not much to ~~t~~ tell you of things here, except, the manoeuvres we were on about a fortnight ago.- it was the hardest time we have had since being in the Durhams marching for practically 3 days with full pack & sleeping in the open, last week from the 17th until the 22nd there was a rifle meeting at Middlewick for the Division I was in for 5 events, but I think it would be best to give up shooting after what I done in them W. O's galore, in some of the competitions the numbers ran ~~to~~ a 1000 competitors, but it was surprising how quickly they were got through, of course they were using the whole of the range. I think I will finish now having exhausted my vocabulary "some word"

With Kind regards
Yours
Dennis

Letter from Dennis [Houseman?] 2.11.17 in Colchester.

276458. B. Coy
Colchester.
2.11.17

Dear Billy
Very glad to hear you are back again in England
+ also that you are not seriously injured + I can
quite understand how glad you must be after going
through what you have, well Billy I have some news
for you this time. first they have made me A1 with
a good few more + they are now making this an
A.1 battalion. all the lower category men, that is B.1
+ below, have been transferred to different regmts
+ they have now made this lot up to full strength +
we are going out as a battalion how long it will be
before we go I have no idea, but they don't appear
to be wasting any time over it, Percy is gone to the
32 London Regmt, at present A+D. Coys are billeted
in empty houses in the town. or at anyrate what is left
of them, the R.S.M. as also volunteered to be made A
Charlie as I believe I told you before is in the R.F.C.
+ if they had waited another fortnight before making
me A I should have been in it as well, my name
came through about 15 minutes before going to
the medical room + of course it is all washed out

now, the capt has gone on his Senior Officers course & he will probably be going to France soon after he as finished it. I suppose you havnt heard anything of Gossling he hasnt written for some little time do you know a fellow named Studleigh who used to be officers servant & was afterward made A he went out with one of the drafts & he is in Glasgow in hospital somewhere whether it is the same one as you I do not know. but if you come across him will you remember me to him & ~~tell him about Charlie, he & Charlie were great~~ pals. there are a lot of fresh officers here now & I am looking after a major Stephens being a A.1. battalion they employ A men now, well, I think this is all for the present so will conclude hoping you are having a good time

Yours as ever

Dennis

I will try & get you Wards home address as soon as I can & let you have it

Letter from Dennis [Houseman] in Colchester 17.11.17.

Colchester.
17. 11. 17

Dear Billy

I'm awfully sorry to have kept you waiting so long
again but I have only just come back off leave not embarkati[on]
& also sorry to say I have not found out poor Will Wards
address yet we have been changing about so much lately
& everyone is new they don't know who I mean & the I seen
the quartermaster & he says go to Bostick, so if he is still here
I will let you have it next week, but Fred Harrison tells
me it is Alcester Rd & over a butchers shop, the butcher is
some relation of Freds, but he doesn't know what number it
is in Alcester Rd. Well Billy how are you getting on are they
trying to make you fit quickly, that is the general rule now
[illegible] shall be pleased to see you once again, but now we
are all A.1. try & keep away from it, there is no knowing
when we shall be going out or where we shall go either.
Freddie Harrison is in D. Coy & is billeted in the town
so it isn't often that I see him. A Coy. are also billeted
in the town. Percy is gone away & is attached to the
32nd London's at Walton on the Naze he has not written
since he went away, but I have his address so I will
give him a gentle reminder when I write. Gosling has

written & is quite well & have been transferred to the ~~Co~~ 6th remember me to Freddie Richardson when you write him again please. Charlie wishes to be remember to you Will close now in a hurry for the post

Kindest Regards

Sincerely Yours
Francis

Letter from Dennis [Houseman?] in Colchester 30.11.17.

Colchester
30. 11. 17

Dear Billy.

Many thanks for your letter of today which I am answering straight away because I have at last got Wards address after a little bit of trouble & it is quite different to what Freddie Harrison told me, it is, 121 Victoria Parade Moseley B.ham. whether this is his mothers address I cannot say, but it is the only address they have of him so Freddie must have made some mistake somewhere. well Billy I'm glad to hear you are going on alright but make it last as long as possible

Gosling wrote me this week he is, up to the time writing, quite well & wishes to be remembered to you. Charlie also wishes to be remembered to you, they aren't half putting him through it & he wishes he was back with us, it seems never ending & to read the papers it looks blacker than ever, especially Russia who might just as well be out of it altogether for what use they appear to be, when you come back here you will be proper Scotch, but it is far different now, to what it used to be we getting better food, sort of fattening us up, but its a braw lot of wee laddies weve gotten now d'ye ken. come off it. I havn't been

to the Baptist but once since you went away, but I will do so & get Mr Hudlestones address for you. I have been going in for amusements, going to the Hip & Theatre each week & it is very nice too. well Billy I will close now with kind regards & best wishes

Sincerely Yours
Dennis

P.S.

Please remember me to L/ Strudly & also Charlie. who would like to hear from him

2Am ~~[illegible]~~ C. D. Edwards ~~R. F. C.~~
276952 R. F. C.
A. R. S
Hut 23
Yatesbury
N. Calne
Wilts

Letter from Dennis [Houseman?] in Colchester 27.12.17.

Colchester
27.12.17

Dear Billy

Just a few lines to see if you are still in the land of the living or whether you received my last letter. How are you going on old boy getting better. I suppose it is jolly cold up there isn't it, here, the snow has been on the ground since Xmas evening. it is quite seasonable. I have taken to coming to the Baptist again, it is so much more sociable here than at the Congregational. last night there was a social here + we spent a very jolly evening

I have Mr. Ludbrooke's address you will find it at the end of this letter. there is not much doing in town now everything is very quiet. I forgot to mention it before, last night they made a presentation to Mr + Mrs Ludbrooke in recognition of their services which they have given so freely, I believe, ever since this place was opened, both Mr + Mrs Ludbrook wish to be remembered to you + as I told them you were likely to come here again they will be extremely pleased

to see you, but Billy keep away if possible, not that I shouldn't like to see you again there isn't anything that would give me greater pleasure, but you have had one visit to France + no doubt you will not relish the idea of another, when is it all going to end it appears to be going from bad to worse, but of course it will come to an end someday + then once more the joys of civil life well good-night old chap, I hope you had a jolly Xmas + I sincerely hope you will have a Happy New Year

+ this year will see the end of this awful business

Sincerely Yours
Dennis

Mr. J. Ludbrooke
43. East St
Colchester
Essex

Letter from Dennis [Houseman?] 13.1.18.

13.1.18 Colchester

Dear Billy

Glad to hear you have received my last letter alright. I was in doubts as to whether you would get it sent on & was tempted to write you again, well Billy I'm sorry to hear you are likely to be pushed out again & so soon & I only wish you were coming here again, for from what I can gather we shall not be leaving here for about a couple of months, but of course you can never tell & as the majority of these fellows are practically strangers, if it comes to going out, I should

ii

like to go out with a few of the old boys. I am jolly glad to hear the good news of Siley, Godd[illegible] & the rest of the boys especially of these two, as we heard they were both killed. To-night, Sun is the first time I have been to town this week, for it is so dark here, there is really no pleasure in going out at night but you get so sick of staying every night, it really does you good to get out. my A.C.1. is due again & I have put in application, don't know yet whether I shall be fortunate

iii

enough to get home again, but all being well I think it will be alright. I should like to hear some definite news of poor Billy Ward, of course there doesn't appear to be much doubt about it, but the girl I used to know at Andover has received news of a fellow who went to France & was reported missing after about 18 mths. the place where you are must be absolutely putrid if it is worse than Catterick, it would be good if you could get here Well Billy, old dear, I will close

iv

now hoping ~~you~~ this will find you quite well as it leaves me at present

Kind Regards

Sincerely Yours

Dennis

P.S.

Please remember me to the boys

Letter from Harold Browne 13.1.1919.

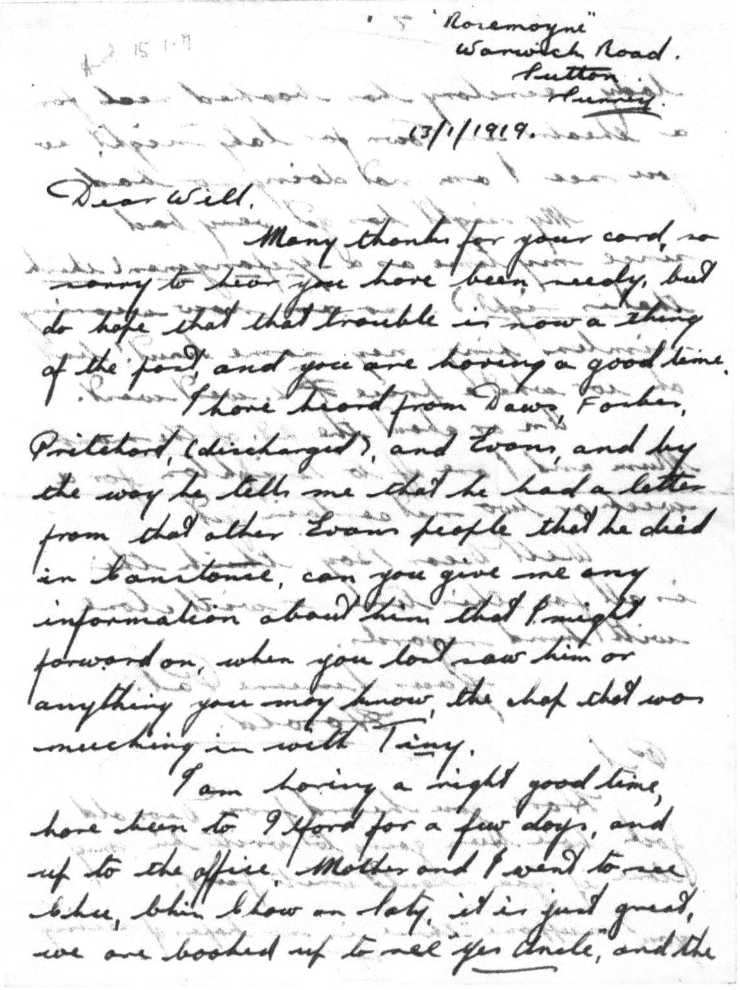

A? 15 1 19

"Rosemoyne"
Warwick Road.
Sutton
Surrey.

13/1/1919.

Dear Will,

Many thanks for your card, so sorry to hear you have been seedy, but do hope that that trouble is now a thing of the past, and you are having a good time.

I have heard from Daws, Forbes, Pritchard, (discharged), and Evans, and by the way he tells me that he had a letter from that other Evans people that he died in [illegible], can you give me any information about him that I might forward on, when you last saw him or anything you may know, the chap that was mucking in with Tiny.

I am having a right good time, have been to Ilford for a few days, and up to the office, Mother and I went to see Chu, Chin Chow on Saty, it is just great, we are booked up to see "Yes Uncle", and the

7.

lady secretary has booked seats for
a theatre in Town for Saty night, so
you see I am not doing so bad.

My sight has got very bad
since my time as a Gefangenen (think
that is right) so am now wearing
rimless fing-ney some kind, but
oh lor what a price £2, went west.

On or about the 28. of the month
Mum and I are off to Brighton for a
week or two not certain yet.

Well Dear Boy, think this
is all for this time so will close
with kind regards.

Your sincere Pal.
Harold.

P.S.

Have you heard from Dear old
Jock, have been going to write him, my
love if you should write first. I
you? suppose there is no hope of seeing

H.

Letter from Harold Browne 30.1.1919.

Ans'd 2.2.19 1.

"Rosemoyne"
Warwick Road.
Sutton.
Surrey.
Jany 30/1919.

Dear Will,

Many thanks for your two letters of the 16 & 28, which I have been going to answer before, so here goes.

As you will see by the post mark, I am at Brighton, got here yesterday, the weather not being too bad, a bit cold.

Thanks so much for trying to get information of poor old Evans, perhaps his people may have had news through from other sources by now.

Tonight we are all going to the Theatre Royal to see The Luck of the Navy.

Yes Dear Boy it is as you say absolutely Top Hole to be free again, and to go just were you like, without having a few sacrements thrown at you.

Yes I shall be jolly pleased to see you when you come up to Town, so don't forget to let me know, we will see if we can fix up a theatre.

2.

Yes Old Chap I think it will be as you say, the army will not trouble us very much now, and I can tell you I am in no hurry to worry them.

Do you know there is a shop down here that sells all kinds of stones and uncut jewellery, this morning I purchased a model of Beachy Head lighthouse in Onyx stone jolly nice, and they have several other things in amythest, and quartz, so I am after them, since I have been back I have got an oriental turn of mind, and got a mania for collecting things.

Well I must now pack up, trusting to hear or see something of you soon, with kindest regards I still remain.

Your Old Pal.

Harold.

C/o Mrs West.
29, Devonshire Place.
Brighton.

The next item may be out of sequence. It is an envelope to Germany from The Midland Hotel, Birmingham where my father was general manager at one time in his career. I thought that this was after WW1 but the date stamp is unclear as it may be either 10th Feb 1914 or 1948. However, because it is in the documents I have included it. My father was born on 21st April 1894 so would have been only nineteen at the time of the earlier date although he could have been a junior member of staff to return later following his time in West Africa on The Gold Coast between December 1919 and sometime in either 1926 or 1927. He married my mother, Amy Eva Bowles on 27th May 1927. Unfortunately, the later date also doesn't fit because in 1948 he was living in Northfield, Birmingham with my mother and me when I was aged three, having been born on 3rd January 1945.

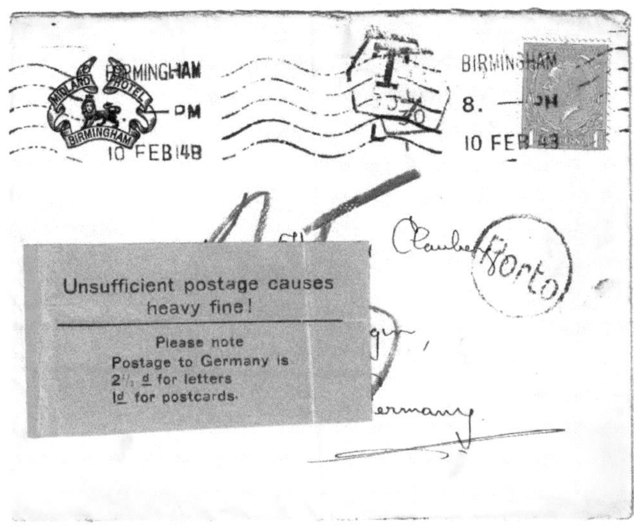

Letter from Harold Browne April 26th 1919.

"Rosemoyne"
Warwick Rd.
Sutton.
Surrey.

April 26/1919.

Dear Will,

I wrote you when you were in hospital, but up to the present have heard nothing of you.

At the time I was in hospital too at my Depot with Valvular Disease of the heart, I was then sent to the heart hospital at Colchester, where I stayed six weeks, and got my discharge on Wed. my official ticket coming this

2

morning.

On Monday shall go up to the office to see what they are going to do with me.

Well Dear Boy have got your ticket yet, and what are you doing.

Last week in Colchester I met a K.R.R. who was at Lichfield, said he saw me giving out the Pay-Book. told me nearly all the old hands had signed on for four years to get the bonus, but I have had enough of it, not to the bonus.

3.

The last I heard of Paddy was, that he was on 30 days leave, looked to me as if he was going to have another trip to the Rhine, I hope not.

Have you been up to Town lately, to any of the theatres?

Well Dear Boy think this is all for now, so close hoping you are well, with kindest regards.

Yours very sincerely.

Harold W. Browne

Letter from Harold Browne August 5th 1919.

Recd 16.8.19

"Rosemoyne"
Warwick Rd.
Sutton.
Aug 5th. 1919

Dear Will.

Many thanks for your letter, I had wondered what had happened to you. and thought you must be out of the army by this time. the last time I wrote you was from Bury St. Edmunds. I think you were in Hospital somewhere.

After leaving Bury I went to Colchester for six weeks for heart treatment and was discharged on April 24th. with a small pension.

I was home for about a fortnight, and then went back to the office, where I have been ever since.

Ah things were very tame here on Peace Day, so cleared off to the Pictures in the evening.

Today Mother & I are going up to Town to see the River Pageant, and then shall probably go on to the Colisseum in the evening.

2.

I have taken up photography lately find it rather an expensive game and not always very good results, must do something with all the money we earn

I heard from Pritchard about a fortnight ago, he send me a photo of the shrine for our chaps in Lichfield. have you got one, if not I will have some copies done, and let you have one.

Pritch is teaching in a school near Gloucester, and likes it very much.

Well Dear Boy must now pack up trusting you are keeping fit, and getting on all right.

Close with Best Wishes, and Kindest Regards.

Yours Very Sincerely.

Harold

Card from the Prisoners of War Reception Committee. [My father has dated it 1918.]

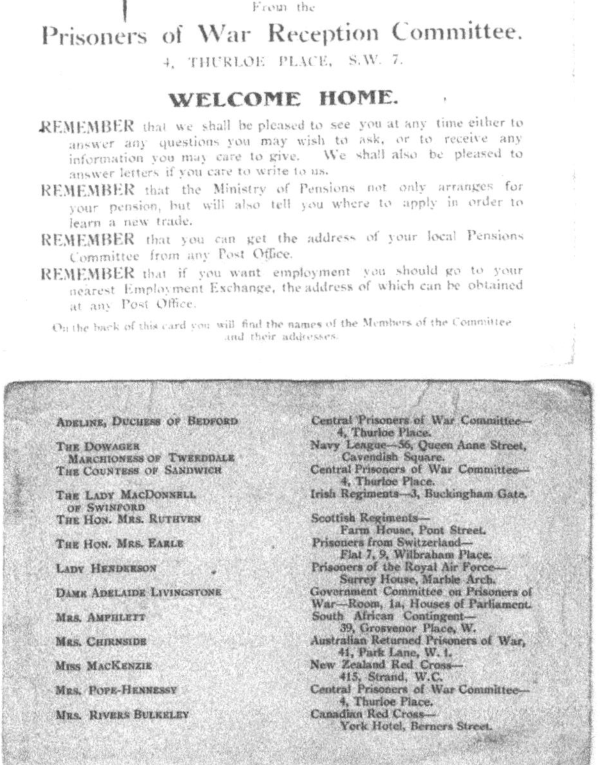

From the

Prisoners of War Reception Committee.

4, THURLOE PLACE, S.W. 7.

WELCOME HOME.

REMEMBER that we shall be pleased to see you at any time either to answer any questions you may wish to ask, or to receive any information you may care to give. We shall also be pleased to answer letters if you care to write to us.

REMEMBER that the Ministry of Pensions not only arranges for your pension, but will also tell you where to apply in order to learn a new trade.

REMEMBER that you can get the address of your local Pensions Committee from any Post Office.

REMEMBER that if you want employment you should go to your nearest Employment Exchange, the address of which can be obtained at any Post Office.

On the back of this card you will find the names of the Members of the Committee and their addresses.

ADELINE, DUCHESS OF BEDFORD	Central Prisoners of War Committee—4, Thurloe Place.
THE DOWAGER MARCHIONESS OF TWEEDDALE	Navy League—56, Queen Anne Street, Cavendish Square.
THE COUNTESS OF SANDWICH	Central Prisoners of War Committee—4, Thurloe Place.
THE LADY MACDONNELL OF SWINFORD	Irish Regiments—3, Buckingham Gate.
THE HON. MRS. RUTHVEN	Scottish Regiments—Farm House, Pont Street.
THE HON. MRS. EARLE	Prisoners from Switzerland—Flat 7, 9, Wilbraham Place.
LADY HENDERSON	Prisoners of the Royal Air Force—Surrey House, Marble Arch.
DAME ADELAIDE LIVINGSTONE	Government Committee on Prisoners of War—Room, 1a, Houses of Parliament.
MRS. AMPHLETT	South African Contingent—39, Grosvenor Place, W.
MRS. CHIRNSIDE	Australian Returned Prisoners of War, 41, Park Lane, W. 1.
MISS MACKENZIE	New Zealand Red Cross—415, Strand, W.C.
MRS. POPE-HENNESSY	Central Prisoners of War Committee—4, Thurloe Place.
MRS. RIVERS BULKELEY	Canadian Red Cross—York Hotel, Berners Street.

Draft of poem entitled: “Mount Edgcumbe Way”, written on notepaper of the Adelphi Hotel And Restaurant. Judging by the handwriting it could be by Harold Browne as it is in black ink but it doesn’t have his precise style nor are many of the letters similar. Therefore, its author must remain a mystery.

TELEGRAMS:
"PHINCHADEL, WESTRAND."
TEL. NO: GERRARD 8481

GEORGE E. FINCH.
PROPRIETOR.

**ADELPHI HOTEL
AND RESTAURANT,**
**JOHN STREET,
STRAND, W.C.2.**

Mount Edgcumbe Way!,
Mount Edgcumbe Way
I truthfully can say
I find no kinder hearted folk than they
~~than they~~ [illegible]
Mount Edgcumbe Way
and they who like things wh. they seen
~~[illegible]~~
~~[illegible] Plymouth Cream~~
not grocers gin but Plymouth Cream
will find the ~~[illegible]~~ a dream
wantside.
First house 'The arms' this as you land,
Last as you leave 'The Hearts and hand'
But meals at either must be planned
He'll get you anything, will Ronsecan
Thats in this line. I know but few so
Very pleased as ~~they~~ all ~~[illegible]~~ to do so.
the ~~[illegible]~~ Hosts Mount Edgcumbe Way

Letter from A. Taylor 10.5.1920.[By this time my father was working on The Gold Coast in British West Africa for H B Russell, an import and export company based in Liverpool. He lived in the coastal village of Saltpond near Cape Coast]

48 Clincart Road
Mount Florida
Glasgow
10/5/20

Dear Robert,

I duly received your very welcome letter, and needless to say I was very pleased to learn that you were keeping well. I had a few lines from Harold Brown at the end of January, and he informed me that you had sailed for the Gold Coast. I was rather surprised to get this news, as I thought you were going to settle down in England, well old chap, I wish you every success in your new venture, and I hope your leg will not give you any further trouble, however, it is annoying to know that the shrapnel is still there.

I suppose you will now be into the ways and customs of your new country, but I know you would find it a bit awkward at first, however, the great experience you had at Lechfeld in buying and selling should now be a decided help to you.

I am pleased to say that I have enjoyed good health since returning to auld Scotland; with the exception of an attack of Lumbago. however, I am now A.1. again.

Business has been very good with me this last year, but we have great trouble in securing materials, in fact paper is costing more now than it did during any period of the war. Sorry the country is in a very unsettled state, the high cost of living has a lot to do with it.

I was very sorry to learn that Harold was troubled with his Heart, but after all, very few people are absolutely sound in this organ.

I dont think I can mention anything else very interesting to you meantime, so I will finish off now, again wishing you good health and luck, and hoping to hear from you soon that like Johnnie Walker you are going strong.

With kind regards from Mrs T and self.

Sincerely Yours. A. Taylor

Roundels from target practise at Colchester 2nd August 1917. [Two sessions, with his comments on the reverse sides.]

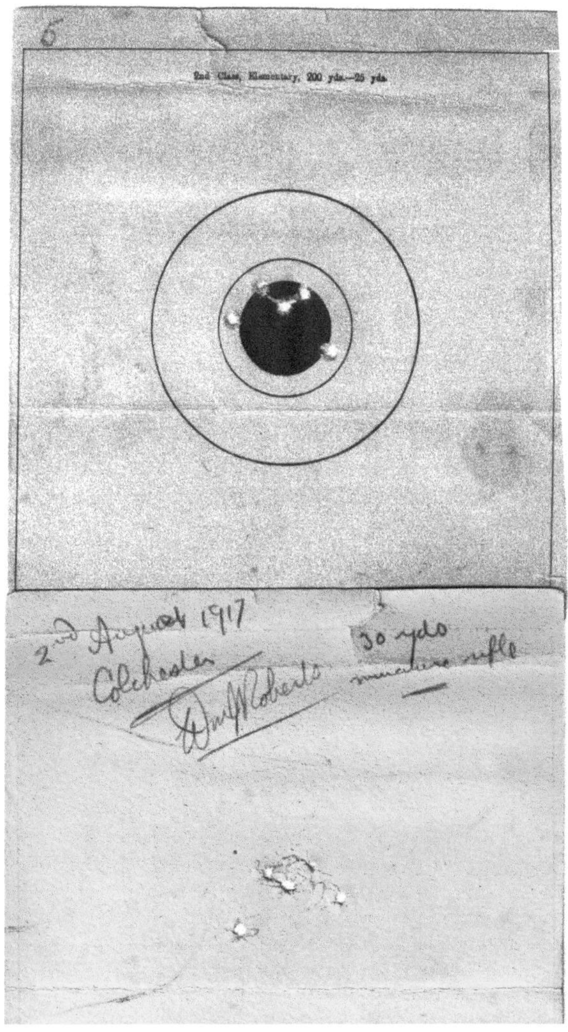

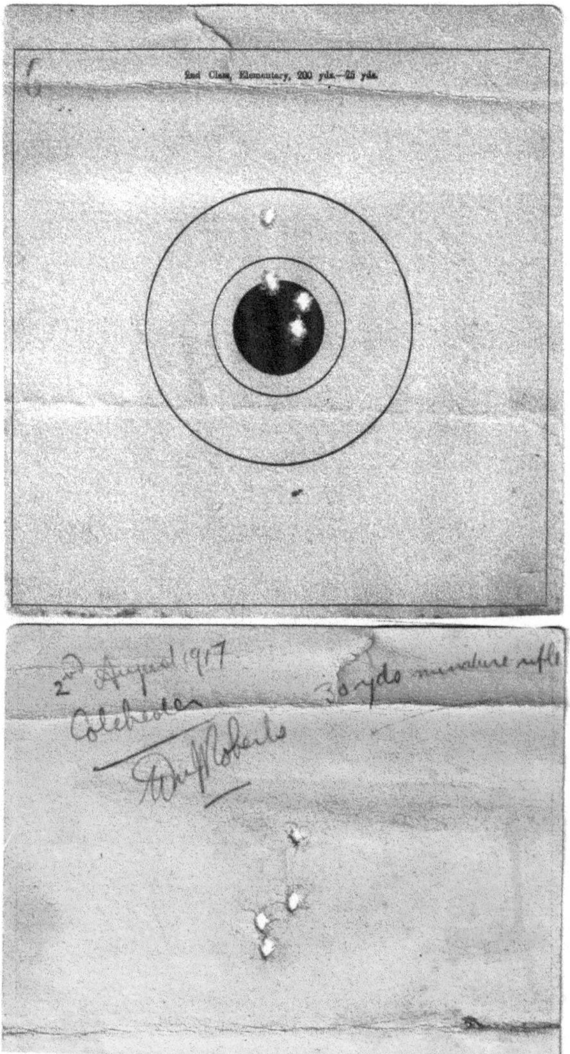
2nd Class, Elementary, 200 yds.—25 yds.
2nd August 1917
Colchester
30 yds miniature rifle

THE PHOTOGRAPHS

Amongst the documents in my father's mementos is a collection of images of his comrades taken during training and [I assume] in the pow camp at Lager Lechfeld. Some benefit from having been annotated either by my father or the photographs' subjects.

1 W. Ward Doncaster. 16.7.1916.

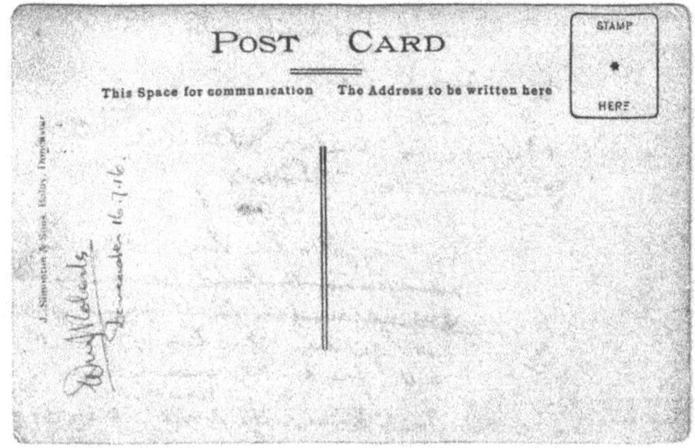

2 My father's platoon. Doncaster. 16.7.1916.

3 More of my father's comrades. Many of those referred to in the diaries and letters are pictured here. Unfortunately, there are no names on the reverse of the post card.

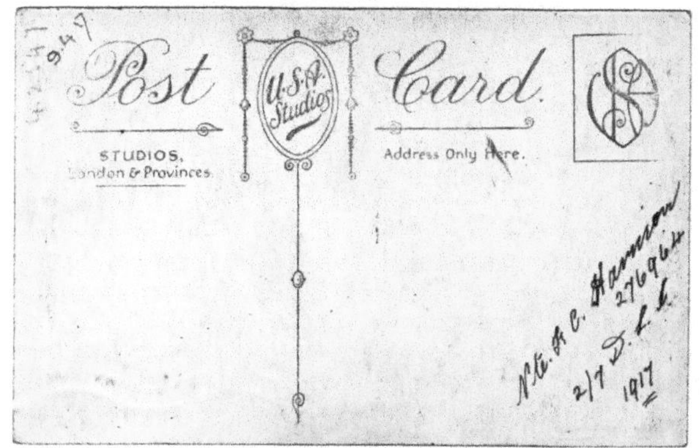

4 Private F(T?)C Harrison. 9.4.1917.

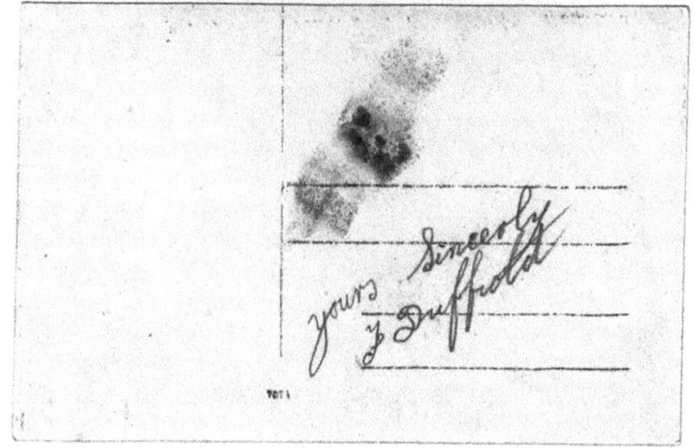

5 Privates with POW armbands. The reverse is signed by F. Duffield.

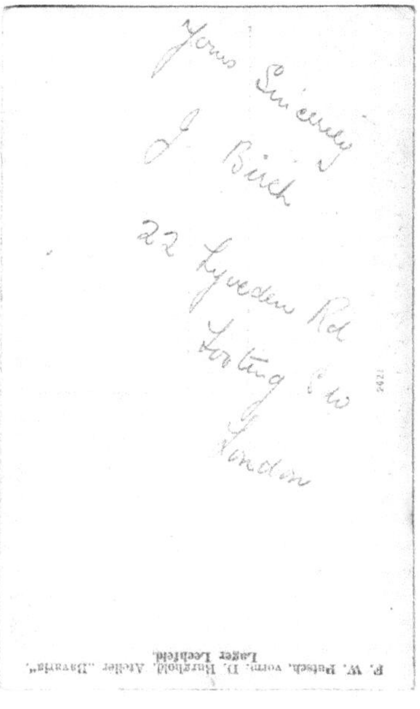

6 J. Birch wearing POW armband.

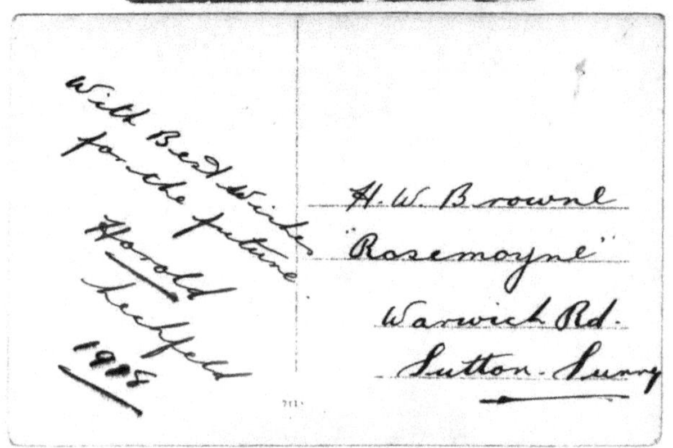

7 H W Browne 1918

8 Eskdale & Stephenson. 5/19.

9 Unnamed Soldier but sure to be one of those referred to in the diaries or from whom my father received letters or post cards. It is worth noting that the pc is printed: Winchester.

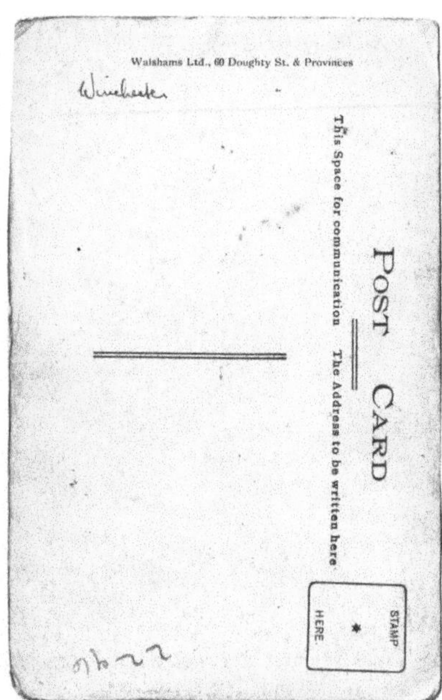

10 Group of Four at Winchester. The man sitting is the same as the last image. (No 9).

11 Private A. Taylor. 1st R S F.

12 Guylian Llawen a Bliyddyn Neydd dda. Annotated Nadrlig 1912. This appears to be written in the Welsh language but I can't be certain. The first two words seem to be the subject's name. The date is two years before the outbreak of World War 1 so the reason for its inclusion is unclear. Maybe he was one of my father's pals from Anglesey where he lived for the first thirteen [at least] years of his life.

13 Private Patrick McGrath [Undated] and Another.

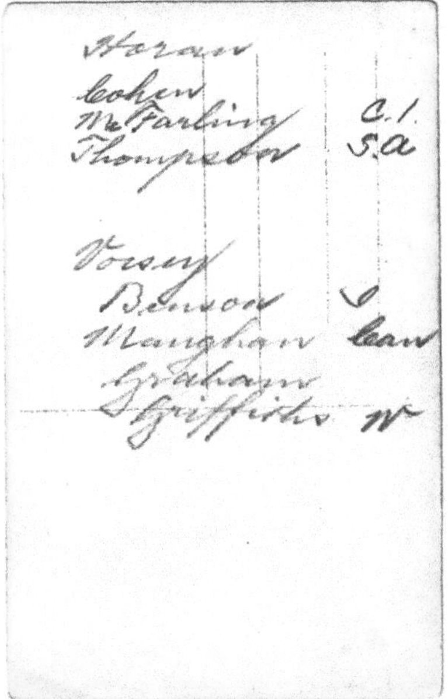

14 Group of Nine. Presumably also at Lager Lechfeld. [Undated]

15 Group of Three at Andover 2/17. These are: D. Houseman, P. Scudamore and A Shell.

16 Ceremony at Lager Lechfeld in the open for what appears to be a funeral/burial.

17 Sargent Scott, Sargent Millward & Self[my father private WJG Roberts] 1919. Presumably at Lager Lechfeld. There is another soldier in the background occupying a doorway. Could he be a German guard or another pow? In which case, why isn't he named?

18 At Dorchester: Borough Gardens 1919. My father is on the right.

Army Form W.5112.

RECORD OFFICE.

York

March 11th 1922.

I am directed to transmit the accompanying British War & Victory Medals which has been awarded to you in respect of your services with the

Durham Light Infantry.

I am to request that you will be so good as to acknowledge the receipt of the decoration on the attached form, which is to be returned to the above address in the enclosed addressed envelope, which needs no stamp.

I am,
Your obedient Servant,

Pte W. J. Roberts

[signature] Major
for Lieut.-Colonel.
i/c. Infantry Records, YORK.

Letter Enclosing His War Medals

Pte. W. J. Roberts

BUCKINGHAM PALACE

1918.

The Queen joins me in welcoming you on your release from the miseries & hardships, which you have endured with so much patience & courage.

During these many months of trial, the early rescue of our gallant Officers & Men from the cruelties of their captivity has been uppermost in our thoughts.

We are thankful that this longed for day has arrived, & that back in the old Country you will be able once more to enjoy the happiness of a home & to see good days among those who anxiously look for your return.

George R. I.

Letter From The King to Private Roberts.

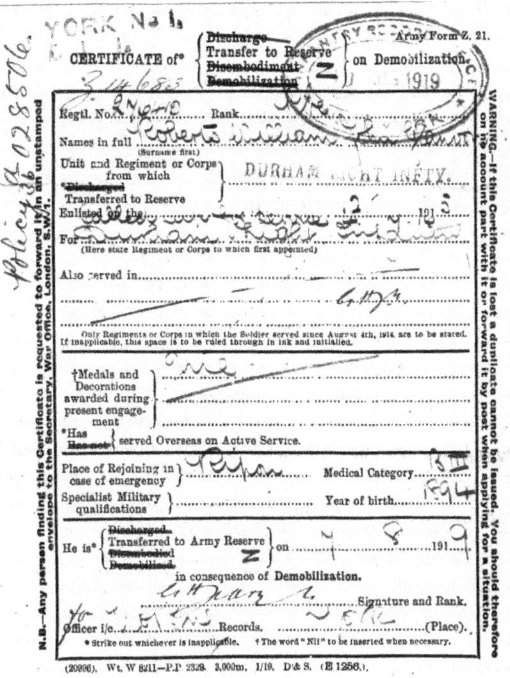

YORK No 1.

Army Form Z. 21.

CERTIFICATE of* ~~Discharge~~ / Transfer to Reserve / ~~Disembodiment~~ / ~~Demobilization~~ Z on Demobilization.

1919

Regtl. No. .... Rank ....

Names in full .... (Surname first)

Unit and Regiment or Corps from which ~~*Discharged~~ Transferred to Reserve ...... DURHAM LIGHT INFTY.

Enlisted on the .... 191 .....

For .... (Here state Regiment or Corps to which first appointed)

Also served in ....

....

....

Only Regiments or Corps in which the Soldier served since August 4th, 1914, are to be stated. If inapplicable, this space is to be ruled through in ink and initialled.

†Medals and Decorations awarded during present engagement ....

*Has / ~~Has not~~ served Overseas on Active Service.

Place of Rejoining in case of emergency .... Medical Category ....

Specialist Military qualifications .... Year of birth 1894

He is* ~~Discharged.~~ / Transferred to Army Reserve / ~~Disembodied~~ / ~~Demobilized.~~ Z on .... 191 .....

in consequence of **Demobilization.**

.... Signature and Rank.

Officer i/c .... Records. .... (Place).

* Strike out whichever is inapplicable. † The word "Nil" to be inserted when necessary.

(20996). Wt. W 8211—P.P 2329. 3,000m. 1/19. D & S. (E 1256.).

N.B.—Any person finding this Certificate is requested to forward it in an unstamped envelope to the Secretary, War Office, London, S.W.1.

WARNING.—If this Certificate is lost a duplicate cannot be issued. You should therefore on no account part with it or forward it by post when applying for a situation.

Letter of Demobilization.

SUMMARY OF SERVICE

Finally, I enclose below a summary of his service prepared by Sean Godfrey. The descriptions of his injuries differ marginally from those which my father mentions in his entries. For example, he refers to shrapnel wounds incurred at the Battle of The Aisne but the medical records do not yet state that he had a gunshot wound to the left knee. This conflicts with earlier references to him having incurred this injury in Polygon Wood. However, the records fix those inflicted in Polygon Wood as 'Gunshot Wounds to Thighs and Head'.

Private 276410 WILLIAM ROBERTS: Documentation

Medal Index Card
Shows that he was entitled to the Victory and British War Medals

Medal Roll of Individuals
Shows the three DLI battalions he served with and that upon discharge he went to Class Z Reserve

Cover For Discharge Documents
Shows that he was discharged to Class Z Reserve (liable to be called up again if required)
Shows that he was with 3rd Battalion DLI which was a Reserve Battalion

Casualty Form – Active Service
Shows old regimental number of 4991 however upon being called up he has been given new number
He left from Folkestone on 06/08/17 posted to 15 DLI
23/08/17 – At Etaples (large base/training camp) with 35 Infantry Base Depot – this is likely to have been to await drafting.
26/08/17 – To 15 DLI
05/10/17 – Wounded and on 06/10/17 to 64 Field Ambulance with 'Gunshot Wounds to Thighs and Head'. Sent on same day to 37 Casualty Clearing Station, then to 20 General Hospital.
15/10/17 – To ship to England
17/02/18 – left Folkestone and on 19/02/18 he was posted to 8 DLI
20/02/18 – To 24 General Hospital with influenza
Illegible until 10/04/18 when back at Etaples
16/04/18 – to 8 DLI

07/06/18 – Reported Missing in the Field

Statement as to Disability
Self explanatory
Gunshot Wound in left knee on 27/05/18 (first day of the Battle of the Aisne).
Suffering also Nervous debility and defective eyesight due to Wo?
Part 9a – Gunshot wound left knee
9b – illegible
12 – less than 20%

Medical History
Examined 04/01/16
Operated for Appendicitis 18 months ago
Slight – rest is illegible until '5t on left (slight)'
'Fit for Garrison Service at Home' is crossed out

Opinion of the Medical Board
21a – 1) Gunshot Wounds left knee and calf
2) Loss of Memory
21b – 1) Temporary. Function apparently not impaired (referring to GSW injuries)
2) Loss of memory for? ? ? – nervous disability (illegible)
23 – 1) Permanent disability (GSW injuries)
2) Doubtful (Loss of memory and nervous disability)

Renewals which have taken place since discharqe
Report of Medical Board 27/05/20
Presents less than 20%

I cannot understand the Award or Decision but I think he received some form of Pension
It says 'GSW Knee' then the rest is illegible until 'from expiration of former award'

Private 276410 William Roberts

12/12/15 – Joined for duty. He is likely to have been a 'Derby Scheme' man. An initiative by Lord Derby for men to sign up and be called up when required. The closing date was 15/12/15. He has then been sent back to civilian life. With his age he should have been called up around February 1916 but he hasn't been called up until 04/07/16. This may have been because his medical category was Bl, he must have had some form of medical issue. Al to A4 categories were for 'General Service' (front line), Bl were fit for 'Garrison or Provisional Units. Fit for service abroad but not for General Service'. If he had gone abroad as a Bl he would have been used to guard HQ's, Supply Dumps, Training Camps etc

04/07 /16 – Called up to 7 DLI. As 1/7 DLI were serving in France he would after training have served with 2/7 or 3/7 (an unusual system of the Territorial forces was that one battalion could have three battalions). As 3/7 were absorbed in Sept 1916 by 3/5, it is likely that he would have served with 2/7 DLI. In Nov 1916 they were based at Andover and in March 1917 they were at Colchester.

06/08/17 – Left Folkestone for Boulogne to join 15 DLI, his medical issue must have improved. I don't think he has joined 15 DLI until around 26/08/17 (it is hard to read). He has first been sent to Etaples, a huge depot used to toughen/ harden up soldiers going to, or returning after wounds to the front line.

Battle of Polygon Wood (Third Ypres)

21 Division of which 15 DLI were part of in 64 Brigade were in the line east of Polygon Wood. 15 DLI were selected for the assault on 4th October.

02/10/17 – 15 DLI drew battle stores from Ridge Wood

03/10/17 – 0130 hours, 15 DLI dug in south east of Glencorse Wood. During the day 15 DLI suffered heavily from German artillery and had to be replaced in the attack by the KOYLI. Casualties were so heavy that 15 DLI survivors were reorganised from four companies into two companies.

04/10/17 – 0600 hours, 64 Brigade attacked in wind and rain with their right on the Hooge-Reutel road. Joist Farm was captured after heavy fighting. A/B Company of 15 DLI were sent up and dug in on the Joist Farm line, south of the farm along the north edge of Cameron Covert by 2pm. The company beat off a fierce German counter attack from the covert. At 9pm, the rest of 15 DLI joined the company.

05/10/17 – Early morning the Commanding Officer of 15 DLI, Colonel Falvey-Beyts organised an attack on a German pillbox that surrendered without a fight. 15 DLI suffered again from shell fire and in the evening the Germans counter attacked, at 11pm Col Falvey-Beyts was killed. 15 DLI were relieved in the early hours of the 6th.

Casualties (killed/wounded) from the 2nd to the 6th were 430 soldiers (approximately 50% of the battalion).

05/10/17 – Wounded with Gunshot wounds to thigh and head and admitted to 64 Field Ambulance then 37 Casualty Clearing Station.
06/10/17 – Admitted to 20 General Hospital, Camiers
15/10/17 – Sailed for England

17 /02/18 – Left Folkestone for Boulogne
19/02/18 – Posted to 8 DLI, (151 Brigade, 50th Division)
20/02/18 – At Etaples and admitted to 24 General Hospital with influenza

The documents are then illegible until:

11/04/18 – At Etaples
16/04/18 – Reported to 8 DLI
8 DLI had taken part in defending against the German offensive on the Somme from 22 March to 1 April losing approx 60% of its strength. They were then sent to the Lys sector to train up replacements when on the 9th the Germans attacked (Battle of the Lys) . 8 DLI were in the thick of the fighting and were relieved on the 13th after losing approx 75% of its strength. From the 15th they began to receive reinforcements, the majority being teenagers and inexperienced. Private Roberts would have been classed as a 'veteran' because he had seen action.
26/04/10 – 50 Division move to the Aisne sector to rest and recuperate.

Battle of the Aisne
The Aisne sector is classed as a quiet sector and was under French command. The British suspected a German attack in this area but the French disagreed. Unknown to the French their 12 Divisions and the 4 British Divisions were to be attacked by 41 German Divisions.

151 Brigade went into the line on 6th May in front of the Chemin des Dames. The area was quiet and peaceful, a nightly chorus of frogs, the beauty of woods, flowers and singing birds. However the British knew an attack was coming. On the night of the 26th, 8 DLI was in the line at Chevreux, the Germans could be seen massing in large numbers. At 1 am on the 27th the German bombardment began and for 3 hours high explosive and gas drenched the British lines, destroying the front line. At 4am the Germans attacked and 8 DLI and the rest of 151 Brigade were overwhelmed. The German report on the battle said that the 151 Brigade survivors of the bombardment fought 'till their weapons were torn from them'. By 5am only isolated posts survived from 8 DLI. The few survivors fell back to the Aisne bridges and a group of 6 and 8 DLI soldiers held back the Germans at Cuiry-les-Chaudardes till

11am. Other survivors held the line of the canal. At midday the remnants were organised and held the heights on the south bank of the Aisne but later fell back to Vantelay and then Jonchery. By the 30th May all that remained of 151 Brigade was 103 soldiers (out of approximately 3000 on the 27th).

All that can be confirmed about 8 DLI on the 27th is that D Company's trenches were levelled in the bombardment and casualties were high. B Company reported at 4.30am that casualties were very heavy but they were holding the Germans up and they would fight to the last, no one escaped. C Company lost heavily, one platoon being completely wiped out, the commander gathered reinforcements and held a defensive position from which no-one escaped.

27 /05/18 – Wounded at the Battle of the Aisne and likely to have been taken prisoner
07 /06/18 – Officially posted as Missing
23/12/18 – Came back to England
07 /08/19 – Demobilised to Class Z Reserve

There are several entries in which my father mentions feeling unwell and which cannot be associated with the wounds he sustained in the fighting. I believe these record his having contracted influenza in the then current global pandemic referred to as 'Spanish 'Flu'. My mother once told me that he also had emphysema resulting from the effects of 'Mustard' [Sulfer Mustard] gas.

THE ARTEFACTS

Helmet and goblet carved during his time at Lager Lechfeld. [They are approximately 15-20mm in length/height].

Phial and Shaving Mirror.

Medal and badge.

His uniform epaulettes, badges, buttons etc., of The Durham Light Infantry.

EPILOGUE

These are two photographs of my father and Amy Eva Bowles who became his wife [and eventually my mother] thought to have been taken around the time of their marriage on 27th May 1927. I believe that the one of my mother was from their honeymoon in Eastbourne where they spent seven weeks. That of my father is probably earlier[possibly 1921] but long after the end of the war when he spent eight years on the Gold Coast of West Africa. I believe that he sailed there with Elmer Dempster Lines in early 1919; possibly on the Appam.

The Appam sailed from Liverpool and he disembarked in Accra where his posting was to represent the Pool's largest world-wide trading company in Africa. Enduring malaria, yellow fever and other local challenges he can truly lay claim to the nomenclature – 'The Great Survivor'.

THE END

CPSIA information can be obtained
at www.ICGtesting.com
Printed in the USA
BVHW021838041021
618136BV00007B/66